MW00619405

Travels on the Yellow Brick Road

Lessons Learned on the Path to Oz

Cathy Weber-Zunker

www.cathysays.com

$20 US / $30 Canada

Travels on the Yellow Brick Road –
Lessons Learned on the Path to Oz

ISBN 0-9728815-0-6 Paperback book

ISBN 0-9728815-1-4 Audio book recording

Copyright 2003 © Cathy Weber-Zunker. All rights reserved.

Printed in the United States of America. No part of this publication may be reproduced, stored in a retrieval system or transmitted in any form or by any means, electronic, mechanical, photocopying, and recording or otherwise, without the written permission of the publisher. For permission requests or to order books, please write Travels, 1217 Fillmore Street, Alexandria MN 56308 or visit www.cathysays.com

Book Design –
Jennifer Winningham designs
www.JenniferWinningham.com

Photography –
Dawn's Touch dawn@runestone.net

With love I dedicate this book

To my mom and dad
Delores and George Ruhland
**I know that if you were here on earth that I would not
need advertising ... all by yourselves the two of you
would tell the world that Travels on the Yellow Brick
Road is ready to read.**

To my sons
John, Robert, and Thomas

**For letting me
... grow with you.
... make discoveries with you.
... look at the world with you.
... write about you.**

To my husband
**Joe Zunker
... the love of my life.
... the warmth in my bed.
... the passion in my heart.**

Acknowledgments

Jennifer Winningham
My thanks for your creativity with my web site and with
TRAVELS ... but mostly my thanks for being so delightful
to work with on a computer to computer basis :)
Jennifer Winningham designs
jmw@jenniferwinningham.com

Andrea Pavlicek
For editing ...
and making sure I put myself in my writing.

Karen Schofield
For correcting errors, editing
and for reading it with your heart.

Forward

We forget years but remember moments. Special moments touch our mind and leave indelible marks on our heart. It is these indelible moments that I seek to capture.

To say that I have never missed a precious moment would be a lie. But each time I write about one on paper, it makes me more aware and watchful for the next time. Now I see them every day. The precious moments of new love and old love, when slipping a hand inside someone else's is enough to send warmth through a body.

Where are the precious moments? Everywhere.
Where are they stored? In hearts.
How long will they last? Forever.
How do we get them? Open our eyes.

Contents

1

I don't expect you to remember the daily people in my life... their names or relationships to me.

As an aid, I have added an information line in small letters under the title of some of the stories.

Now... sit back... be ready to laugh... cry... and think.

Welcome to my world...

- Cathy

Good Morning World!

Some mornings ... the beauty of life is just too much to bear. To let it pass without acknowledgment would be a sin! On such glorious days ... when the new day is dawning ... when I step outside I can feel the excitement inside of me ... it's building.

Before I get to the van, I look at the sky and walk with arms spread wide. (Feeling like Julie Andrews at the top of the Sound of Music mountain)

Without hesitation the words explode, "GOOD MORNING, WORLD!"

I have acknowledged the magnificence of the day and life can now move forward.

The peace and quiet of our country yard is the perfect

place for greeting the day this way.

The situation is quite different in the city.

The Place: Tucson, Arizona.
The Time: Taking the days' first step out the front door.
The View: Breathtaking. Desert mountains and pure sunshine.

A glorious day! I am about to embark on a great adventure with my 5-½ year old perfect grandson.

I look around at the pavement, the concrete, the cars, and the townhouses ... knowing that this is NOT the privacy I am accustomed to for greeting the world. But the beauty is winning over self-consciousness. The power behind the beauty is subtle, like the power of a dam holding back a river. With arms spread wide, looking up at the sky, I yell, "GOOD MORNING WORLD!" in a long emphatic sing songy verse.

Brady is watching me in disbelief. You can see the wheels of his mind working. The look on his face says 'You can do that? ... then I can too'. He takes a breath and cautiously projects "GOOD MORNING WORLD". A grin of pure joy slides across his face.

It's my turn again. I lean back, arms spread out wide, with a heart and soul announcement to the world. I once again emphatically proclaim, "GOOD MORNING WORLD!"

Brady's grin grows even wider and this time he is ready. His expression is saying 'O.K. ... now I've got it!' This time the little man, reaches for a huge breath of air ... throws his arms out, head back and hollers his greetings to the day. "GOOD MORNING WORLD!"

He can learn all the lessons of business and work from someone else ... I want to teach him about looking at the world ... rose colored glasses? I wouldn't have it any other way!

Take Me Out to the Ball Game

(7-16-1999: Tom, 18 years old)

It was a hot Friday night in July ... Tommy's last regular season baseball game. All was quiet in the bleachers except for a few casual conversations among team parents.

Top of the fourth ... down by five? How did this happen?

I watched and listened to the people in the stands. I decided that I needed to be involved – to really care – and to let it show. I needed to help pull this team to the positive side – we were down by five – and the feeling in the stands was dismal – impending doom. This was bull! And I say so ... out loud ... calling for double plays ... base hit! base hit! ...

There was a change in the crowd – "hey...yah...this isn't out of hand yet – sure, they can pull off a double play."

Slowly the crowd got involved. There was a coach from another team in the stands. He was watching me and noticing the ever-increasing noise coming from the crowd. Finally every play was being closely scrutinized by the fans – idle conversation stopped … we were part of it … we were on the field … living it.

Tom was on base and had been given the signal to slide. I don't *want* him to slide – he already had leg wounds – but he slid and reopened last weeks' injuries. He loves to play in a uniform with blood on it – it's a guy thing for sure.

The gap in the score was closing steadily.

The opponent had loaded the bases … Tommy was brought in to pitch.

From the stands I was tense with the responsibility that has been given to my son. The task was to come in and pitch the final out of the inning, get the team off the field, and back to the hitting side of the game.

There he stood … with his team, the coaches, the fans – the whole world watching this one young man on the mound. Four pitches later he confidently walked off the mound back to the dugout. And me? I screamed "YES!! YES!!" along with the rest of the group.

I know these four pitches — this one small victory will not win or lose the game … I don't care about winning or losing the game. What I care about is much more important than any game … I want this small victory to add one more drop to Tom's bucket of self-confidence for the future ... so that someday ... when he's walking into the most important test of his life, he will look back and say "Yah, I remember a time when the coach put me on the mound with bases loaded – gave me a chance to be a hero – and I did it – and I'll do it again today."

Did we win the game?
No ... but YES ... because we lived it together.
Did we win the game?
No ... but YES ... because after two extra innings only one point separated the winners from the winners.

A Girl's Best Friend

(20 degrees below zero)

It didn't seem like anything out of the ordinary when Joe asked to use my vehicle for the day. His truck was having repairs and I would be doing child care all day ... not a problem for him to use the van.

That afternoon when he returned with my van he was smiling. He told me he had a surprise for me. I had to shut my eyes and open my hand. In my hand he placed my van keys ... hmmm ... on my key chain was a small black oval shaped device with several buttons on it. I had no idea what it meant.

He explained that his truck didn't need repairs at all. He had *really* taken my van to an electronics store to have an automatic starter installed. There were other gifts he had in mind for this holiday season ... some more romantic than a starter ... but he felt that on a day-to-day basis –

this was the perfect and practical gift. He informed me that the device came with a LOCK – UNLOCK feature so that I would lock my vehicle regularly.

A statement from the Surgeon General should warn of this item's addictive capabilities. A warm vehicle in winter ... heaven ... simply heaven ... to be able to start it from the check-out counter at Wal Mart ... it sounds like such a little thing, but the wide open parking lot with the wind whipping around, feels like the coldest place in town.

After Christmas one night I went to dinner with a couple of girlfriends. It was a frigid evening ... projected to be 20 below before the night was over. I put snow pants & boots in my vehicle ... just in case I might need them. Joe handed me my cell phone as I walked out the door.

At dinner the three of us talked and laughed for hours ... months had gone by since we had seen each other ... we shared our news ... work ... families ... husbands ... our lives. I told them about my car starter. One of the others had just gotten an anniversary ring from her husband. We ooh-ed and aah-ed over the size and magnificence of the stones and settings. Diamonds ... always a girl's best friend.

The night got late. We made promises to get together again soon, but we knew it wouldn't happen ... it's always months in between ... maybe that's what keeps the gathering so special.

We hadn't paid attention to the weather. Stepping outside into the wind and sleet … you could tell without checking the weather channel, the temperature had dropped considerably. After a hug we each ran to our vehicles to get out of the prickly sleet that was sharp on our faces. I hopped into my vehicle … sat there a minute, letting the heat warm my hands and feet.

I looked at the snow pants and boots still laying on the seat beside me … a gift from Joe last year. I looked at the windows nearly cleared of ice. My cell phone was fully charged. Despite 20 below temperatures … I could feel the huge protective arms of my husband wrapping around me. I drove home that night saying thank you to Joe … for not getting me diamonds.

Basketball Court

That old rickety garage had been leaning to the west forever. An outhouse was built into the back corner ... with its own entrance ... not from inside the garage but directly from the back yard. It was classy in its day ... not just one hole but a two holer. (I know people who have side-by-side vanity sinks, but I don't know *anybody* who has a   conversation area with side-by-side toilets as a seating configuration.) The garage was easy to demolish – too easy, it was rotten actually. In a day it was hauled away, leaving no sign that it ever existed.

There were big plans for this area. A basketball court was being built here. This was our first project of the spring. My husband wanted to know how big it needed to be. I had explained that the court *had* to be at least 19 feet and 3 inches ... enough room to shoot a three-pointer.

After preparing an area for concrete Joe invited me to look at the site. I stood watching as he pointed to one tiny corner of the proposed court. Looking at the spot he stated, "Right here, honey. If the boys stand right in this spot – this is exactly 19 feet 3 inches from the basket."

Uh ooh, how was I going to tell him? Very quietly I explained. "The three-point line on a basketball court goes 19 feet 3 inches in a semi-circle *around the basket.*" When he realized the size I was suggesting he asked incredulously, *"Do you know how big that court will have to be?"* I hesitantly suggested that maybe this court needed to be about forty feet? I would settle for nothing less than 40 feet of concrete. This first project of the spring had just doubled in size ... he rented excavating equipment.

The project attracted friends and neighbors ... nobody came to work, of course ... just to visit ... to help pass the time while they *watched us work.* After all: if the neighbors didn't stop by to actually ask you what you were doing ... all of the friends-of-the-neighbors would have to stop *over themselves* to find out what was going on – so in the long run, it's a great time saver to have the neighbors visit.

Men who were total strangers would stop to talk if they saw Joe outside ... I knew when they walked in the yard that they would be leaving disappointed. They had probably been watching the progress using the 'drive-by' method. Then ... when their curiosity was at its limit they would come in the yard to find out exactly what kind of huge garage Joe was building. The 'tail-tucked-between-the-legs' posture was inevitable, as the visitor left the yard in mourning. 40 feet of concrete and it's NOT for a garage ... how sad!

When it was finished the men passing by were disappointed it wasn't a garage – but our half grow-men were thrilled. The back yard became filled with young guys throwing their shirts in the grass on hot summer days – playing basketball until the sweat had soaked everything or until the pizza was ready – whichever came first.

The court had heavy use for just a few years. I can hear the 'garage-lovers' of the world asking why did she have to have a basketball court in their back yard? After all, there's a basketball court just three blocks away, down at the American Legion.

I had to have a basketball court in my back yard ... because I ... wanted to capture the moments. I wanted the boys to bring their friends to our house ... to have pizza at our house ... to play ball in our yard ... to relax and talk smart where I could hear ... I wanted to watch them grow ...

The boys are grown up and gone now. The forty feet of concrete sits empty ... but not long ago I saw John lifting Brady high enough to make a basket ... it won't be long ... it'll be in use again soon.

A Donut Afternoon

Each afternoon mom and dad drove to the bakery in Cold Spring. They bought a roll and coffee ... then parked by Super Value ... ate their treats ... and watched people come and go.

In the hustle of my busy young life, I silently scoffed at their daily routine. My perception of their afternoons falls into the category of being a time waster.

I looked at it differently when I saw them become frustrated with their inability to transport themselves after dad got sick. They no longer could shop for their own necessities – to enjoy the simple pleasure of traveling together... just the two of them.

I watched mom cry one afternoon as dad laid in the living room in his hospital bed. All she wanted was an afternoon drive ... to get a donut ... with my dad. A simple request that was impossible to fulfill ... any one of the kids could have taken them where they wanted to go, but it wouldn't have been the same.

If they argued about medical decisions I thought it was signs of weakness in their relationship ... what a fool I was ... I thought I knew so much about people and life. Their disagreements had nothing at all to do with the underlying foundation ... there was a bond between the two of them that couldn't be broken if the powers of heaven and hell came together.

Mom had ceaseless energy caring for dad ... many hours a day ... nights without sleep ... the demands ... how did she find the strength? Shrugging her shoulders she stated with unequivocal certainty "Well ... I know he'd do it for me."

The donut afternoon was a comfortable part of their day ... two people together ... they often didn't talk about anything ... now I realize ... mom and dad were talking all the time ... I just couldn't hear it.

Gordy

She was a doll of a child – always happy – really she was!

The most even-tempered child I had ever helped to raise. There are three things you need to know about Kristine.

1) When Kristine was little she loved a movie about Gordy the Pig

AND

2) Kristine's dad always loves to sing with the girls.

AND

3) The family's religious affiliation is Catholic.

Put these three items together in one little girl.

Kristine was sitting at the table humming and coloring and coloring and humming. Unable to hold it back any longer, she burst into song " Gordy! Gordy! to God in the highest!"

A Different Choice

Does the elimination of a marriage contract automatically put into effect another decree? Does it legislate a new commitment? This time a commitment to hate someone else for the rest of your life rather than to love? Does a divorce put a permanent bag of garbage on your back? Something that you can and must carry with you for time and all eternity? An uninvited entity, seeking to further its' own cause.

My ex-husband and I made a different choice. We refuse to drop the arched arms of London's Bridge and embrace HATE as 'my fair lady'. Had we let it in, HATE would have created a life of its own.

It generally rattles people, makes them uncomfortable, when they see two human beings who used to be married, conversing comfortably and sharing highlights of their now separate lives.

It baffles people when I tell them that my ex-husband is my most enthusiastic cheerleader of my mothering skills. Always supportive ... and if not in agreement with the course I've taken – always finding a way to make it sound positive – "Wow, that's really a creative solution to this particular problem!" he might say. He has supported me when I've had to say hard things to the three sons that we created together a long time ago. And he *should* be the one supporting my parenting skills ... because we are both pulling in the same direction. And I, in return, am overwhelmingly honest and appreciative of the life lessons he has taught our sons. Lessons in confidence and self-esteem that will escort them along through every step on the path to Oz.

To have a camaraderie like this speaks volumes about the people we each chose as a partner. For surely, if our spouses were not open minded, accepting and willing to build a friendship, then none of this philosophy would work.

But it *does* work.

Years ago, for a class reunion, there was a questionnaire sent out that was going to be compiled into a booklet for each classmate to take home with them. One of the questions on the form was: What is one of the things you are most proud of? ... I didn't think people would understand. I am still disappointed in myself that I didn't answer that question with honesty. The answer? I am most proud of the interaction between two people who were once married ...

... who chose to show their children another way.
... who chose to create a friendship with depth.
... who chose to consciously deny hate as a companion.

A Valentine Gift

Two days of being up earlier than usual. I am preparing to spend a day in the hustle and excitement of Valentine's Day at a floral shop. Me? I'm a volunteer. I just want to help out and take orders – I want to laugh with the last minute orders from guys and husbands – take notes for the cards to be enclosed – the messages, the thoughtfulness ... the romance! An all around chatty day of smiles is what I had in mind.

And then it happened...
In the middle of the afternoon...
Right after school...

A little boy inquired about buying something – something special for his mom – from his pocket he took $1.30. It's store policy ... no child leaves empty handed ... no matter how much money they have.

As he was leaving the shop, his sadness shows … and he mentions to the woman that his mother is dying of cancer … his eyes … his eyes said it all … this was going to be the last Valentine's Day the little boy would ever have to give flowers to his mother. The woman who waited on him returned to her workstation with tears streaming down her face. Soon we all were crying over our flowers.

My niece, the owner, through her tears said, "Go get him back! Go get him!" In a moment someone was running outside to get the child back to the shop – there was quick conversation - an address was taken - and a promise of more flowers was given, they would be delivered today for his mother with his name on the card.

Through my tears I asked my niece, which flowers were being sent – she nodded and gestured with her head – over on the counter awaiting delivery … sitting there … were a dozen red roses in a vase overflowing with baby's breath.

Today is my first Valentine's Day without my mom – no one to take flowers to – and I didn't realize … or couldn't realize … how much I would miss it when she was gone. I turned to my niece and asked "So did *you* send flowers to *your* mom?" She looked at me incredulously and then at the tons of greens that had been shaved from thousands of flowers. Our eyes locked and the face of a little boy returned.

My sister got roses for Valentine's Day.

Richard

Joe and I were quietly eating dinner ... chatting with a guest ... when the front door banged open ... without knocking ... there was Ole. His booming voice filled the house instantly. Ole always made himself at home in the neighborhood ... used a four wheeler to get from house to house. The four-wheeler was convenient ... he could carry a few beverages with him on particularly hot days.

But it was cold out now, so his truck was idling in the driveway. He told me to go change my clothes; he had something I had to see. Joe and Ole talked while I got into sweats ... a minute later I was ready to go. I knew where we were going but I didn't know why yet ... I could hardly wait!

We drove less than a quarter of a mile to Richard's house. Ole's booming Swedish voice, quieted slightly as we entered Richard's home, without knocking, of course.

Richard had a baby bird ... a sickly one ... in an ice cream pail near the heater. At the bottom of the pail was a plastic bag filled with warm water. On top of that was a soft terry towel folded double for softness ... on top of that went the sick bird ... on top of that went another towel over the pail to keep the warmth inside. The little thing fit in the palm of one of my hands.

Ole knew I'd want to see it. He knew that Richard's lifestyle intrigued me ... his peace ... contentment ... his oneness with the land and the animals. Hidden away in a private corner of the world, Richard is one of those people who walk to a different drummer.

A ton of corn a week is quietly delivered to his hide away. All varieties of birds are invited to dinner ... the deer usually invite themselves.

I go to Richard's when the world gets crazy. I know that at Richard's, just like the birds, I am accepted just the way I am.

The bird that Ole took me to see, died. Life and death are both part of the world that Richard inhabits. The land is consistent with his mission in life. A lake hidden from the public for his geese and ducks ... a grove that gets thicker each day ... the trees refusing to let the world take a peek inside ... people pass by ... not knowing that he cares for God's injured creatures ... not knowing that he's on a mission from God.

Bulla

A large group gathered at the airport gate. Lots of kids ... all boarding first, so that they'd be *really* crabby by the time the flight took off. (I have never understood the logic behind boarding children first. Making a child's flight the longest time confined to a seat.) Joe was asking what our row number was and I told him 23A and 23B. The airplane was nearly full as we headed toward the back – in seat 23C stood an adorable six-year-old boy.

After we were seated, the little boy went across the aisle with his mom and brother while the father took the seat next to us. About half way through the flight the two parents switched places. Josh, the six-year-old had a friend along to help him with the three-hour flight.

Josh sat patiently and quietly across the aisle. Lying in his lap was a plain looking stuffed animal ... well ... it *used* to be a stuffed animal at one time. Remember the Velveteen Rabbit? A bunny loved so well, it eventually became real. This animal has been loved so much that he too was getting close to becoming real.

The remains of this little brown animal had features that, with a little imagination, could be construed as a dog once upon a time. The seam was gaping open where the neck and body were supposed to join. Following the natural neckline of the animal was a string going from one side of the gaping neck to the other – it was still intact. I know it was connected because I watched him twirl his finger constantly and contentedly in this thread.

In my mind's eye, I can see this dog some day sitting on a shelf, in the corner of a bedroom watching proudly over a young man in cap and gown. The puppy standing tall and proud of his lack of fur.

With Josh's mom sitting next to me, I asked her to tell me the story of the beloved dog with the exposed stuffing. She smiles and says, "Oh, I don't know, it's sort of like that dog was *meant* to be with us." She explained that the nearly hairless dog had suffered the extremes of being lost in a snowstorm as well as being burned on a stovetop, but had always survived to be protector of this little boy.

When Josh was two, he and his mother and the dog (named Bulla) went to a Twin Cities shopping mall on a snow-stormy Minnesota day. On the way home they realized that the dog was gone. She is a great mom. She began the search for the missing part of the family – for indeed, if the dog remained lost, mom would have cried harder and longer than anyone else.

The search continued in spite of the snow and blizzard conditions. She went back to the mall, a huge place, to the same entrance they had used hours earlier. She randomly asked a stranger, who was walking in the mall for exercise, if he had seen a stuffed dog. Well, as a matter of fact he had ... he thought for sure it must belong to someone who was going to the laundromat next door. He proceeded to put it in the laundromat, high up on top of a washer. And ... there it was.

Now, this man said that he walks at that mall every day – he *never* goes to his car until he's finished walking ... but *that* day ... he took an item to his car ... when he was returning to the mall, there was Bulla laying in the snow.

As best as I could, I've tried to relate the details that the mom gave me. I'm sure it's not all accurate, but the feel of the event is correct – it settles deep in the heart of a child.

This is a dog destined to be with a boy – not just any boy – a boy targeted for greatness ... mark my words.

The Fragrance of Manure

A fragrance crosses your nose. It immediately brings back a memory ... like cookies or apple pie in the oven or fresh baked bread.

Some memories are good and some, not so good. A smell, for me, that always brings with it a warm cozy feeling is the smell of cow manure.

Now, people who have lived in the city all of their lives can't distinguish between cow manure and pig manure or the fragrance of turkeys. But certainly anyone who has experienced country living knows the difference between the scents. We lived in the country. I say we lived in the country instead of saying we were farmers, because we weren't farmers. Dad had a job in the granite quarries and only raised cows for milk.

I remember the cows because my dad broke his ribs. No the cows didn't do it, but it brought me closer to the cows because his ribs were broken. The broken ribs were the reason I was prodded out of bed early on dark winter mornings. Dad could no longer haul the tubs of silage into the barn by himself. I was a small thing at the time, but able to lift one side of the galvanized wash tub well enough to take the pressure off his load.

The silage lay on the ground in a long pile, like the long white plastic silos I see laying on the ground near farmer's barns these days – only without the garbage bag wrapper. Dad would begin digging into the frozen pile of silage every morning and evening. As he dug the steam would roll out of the middle of the pile. Dad would say, "Step in there" – where the warmth was. There he would tuck me into the corner of silage protected from the wind. I watched as he shoveled until the tub was only half full. With him on one side of the tub and me on the other side, we went back and forth to the barn until the morning job was finished. Each trip back to the pile, he protected me from the cold.

The smell of manure … brings back a peaceful cozy feeling from a day gone by … a day of a small girl and her young dad, building a lifelong friendship, one smelly step after another.

Can't Paint, Can't Write, Can't Sing

The things we say to ourselves!

When I find a new self-help, self-awareness, self-improvement book, I can read them fairly quickly. Many of the points are things that I've studied and thought about before. So in the process of reading and doing the writing exercises in the book called Self Matters, there weren't a lot of new ideas ... very common-sensical – step by step ... exercises ... a logical thought process ... and then BAM! I didn't even see it coming! I started putting all of my written assignments together. My positive self-talk wasn't as positive as I thought it was. Frankly, I was stunned. The conversation went like this: "My self talk is positive all the time! I am not being negative when I say to myself that I'm not artistic ... for me, it's just the plain truth ... I just *can't* paint!"

The conversation in my head about writing went like this: "I know that I'm a speaker, but a speaker is something entirely different from writing – with writing you have to use words for every ounce of feeling – and I can't use words ... I use my facial expressions and body language. I *can't* write!"

Same thought process with singing "I *can't* sing."

Now that I had the 'aha' moment of discovery what was I going to do about it?

Well ... I bought paints ... I started on a wall, behind a door ... without anyone knowing. That piece of wall has about 20 pounds of paint from all the times I got frustrated and had to cover up my frightful attempts. Now I have painted murals on walls and practically turned my world upside down with paint ...

One very tiny bathroom in our house never got used – it was so ugly! Who would want to sit in it? I painted this little room sky blue and then proceeded to turn the walls into a tropical island. There is a hideous PVC pipe that runs up the wall that is camouflaged now as a palm tree. The room is complete with an aqua-blue ocean, a sand beach, an umbrella, a cruise ship coming into port, and a bucket of Corona sitting in the sand. A miniature hammock holds a spare roll of toilet paper. Two strips of oak create an enclosed space on the floor around the back side of the toilet and that three-inch deep area is now filled with white beach sand! Guess what? This tiny bathroom gets used now and my husband has been trying to convince me that I should paint professionally!

I discovered that I have always been able to paint, 'knowing' it inside, has changed my entire world.

After painting ... is writing. My book is scheduled to be in print by March.

Singing: In reality everyone can sing! Not only that ... studies have shown even if you just sing with the radio, you improve. I received from my sister a beautifully framed piece of artwork that says, "Use what talents you possess. The woods would be very silent if no birds sang except those that sang best."

Now I sing all the time – with the radio, with CDs ... with or without music. And someday ... someday I might just test those wings, too ...

"Laugh, laugh, laugh!"

When I was thirteen I got home from school one day, very happy. My mom was in the kitchen. I was talkative and excited. I shared with Mom a funny incident that happened in class. I don't remember what it was that was so comical, but I remember vividly the feel of the slap ... not a physical slap, but a slap nonetheless. My mother stood at the kitchen counter. Her teeth were clenched when she said "Laugh, laugh, laugh! Is that all you do? School is for learning, not for laughing."

A hurt can teach us life lessons in a moment, that otherwise could take a lifetime to learn. Hurts can teach us what we don't *ever* want to Say, Do, or Be.

In that moment, I learned several things very quickly.

First: I promised myself to never tell my mother about my life again.

Second: I decided that my children would never feel the sting that I felt that day.

Third: I decided my personality would be nothing like hers.

Fourth: I learned that ... even though she hurt me ... I still loved her deeply.

49

Loving Mom

My sister, Carol, was asked to take a woman named Dawn Christmas shopping this year … it was part of a 'hand-up' organization. Just fourteen days earlier our mother had died. It would have given my sister a justified reason to decline, but she kept the commitment. Giving to others is high on her list of priorities.

As they were shopping together Dawn told Carol that she had been on drugs and alcohol for years … she had five children. She got a divorce and went to rehabilitation … got her life straightened around … got a job … then … started to backslide until she lost her job and two of her children. Now, once again, she is trying to get back on top.

In the course of their morning together my sister told Dawn that our father died just a few months ago and now just two weeks ago our mother died. Our mom had been a difficult person to love. Some troublesome questions haunted all six of us kids – did our mom love us? Why did she have to be so difficult? What happened in her life that made her so cruel? Why wouldn't she let her children love her? What was inside of her that she tried so hard to not let anyone see?

Dawn listened quietly while Carol spoke.

When Carol was finished, Dawn gave her a detailed description of her own mother. Dawn said that her mom was an alcoholic … that her mom drank so heavily that she had a 'water brain' … her mom was now a living vegetable. She said that her mom physically pushed them away if they ever reached for physical comfort … then she turned to Carol and said, "I would have *loved* to have had a mom like yours."

Some days you *think* you are the giver…

Lexy

Lexy was a gorgeous miniature collie – a downsized Lassie.

She was tied up most of the time – which is the terrible fate of an animal that lives in town. Lexy would bark constantly just for the exercise, I suppose, or to overcome boredom. Gentle as she was, it would have been very easy to let her wander the neighborhood.

One sunny summer afternoon, the unspeakable happened – Lexy had gotten off her leash. She was rarely more than a couple blocks from home and always accompanied by a human on a rope. We had no way of knowing which direction she went.

Lexy was on the loose – alone – where to look?

Several minutes later Lexy came around the corner of the

house with ……….. an ice cream cone in her mouth ……
guiltily looking up at me she laid it on the cement. I could
see it all in my mind's eye. A child, outside with a cone in
their hand … Lexy quietly … allowing the child to pet her.
Lexy turns toward the child, gently mouths the cone and
walks off with it. I know that's how it happened … I had
watched her 'killing me softly mode of operation' before.

Guilt was written across her face as the ice cream melted on
the concrete. I said to her "Well, you've got it now – you
might as well eat it …" and she did.

Somewhere … there was a child going back to the kitchen
… asking for a second ice cream cone … trying to explain
that a dog came and took the first ice cream cone right out
his hand. An older sibling walks through a doorway and
shouts "Ya! Right! If he gets another one, then I DO TOO!"

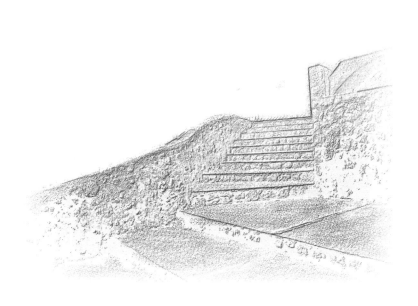

Where Is Color?

(John / 5 years old)

Where is color? In the skin or in the heart?

Sunday morning devotion ... a gathering of people who believe, act, and worship the same. A visiting family arrive ... their skin isn't the same color as everyone else's skin. It's black, not soft brown, but truly black.

They have children ... I have children.

Side by side we study and learn. My five-year-old son is sitting next to a large black woman who has enormous lips. Emphasizing the size of her lips is bright orange lipstick.

My son sits more quietly than usual, with a stranger next to him – someone who may not be patient with his fiddling ... and so he is docile today.

I leave with relief, having received no blatant questions from my sons, who had never seen anyone with different colored skin before.

I kept quiet on the trip home that day ... waiting for the answer to my unasked question. What does a child see looking at a human being with a different color of skin?

On the way home, my son John said, "Hey mom? Ya know that lady sitting beside me?" I said 'yes'. He said, "I *really liked* her lipstick!"

There is no color in the eyes of a child ...

The Messenger

I didn't plan to let the story affect me! I was just reading ... looking for a story with a particular point for a particular presentation. I wasn't looking for anything that would *teach* me anything! The story about an 'umbrella lady' appeared innocent enough. A woman who sent umbrellas to help ease other people's suffering. A protection from the rain and wind of life. Great analogy - great story – wonderful message - very nice ... I'll catalog it in my computer file for possible future use. Over and done.

The next morning was a dark day. Rain. Not just a little rain – buckets of water. The air chilled me to the bone.

I went to town to work on a computer file, determined to stay inside for the duration of the day ... it was nasty outside. Best to even stay away from the windows.

There was a nagging inside of me that day. It would not let me go! A nagging to go and buy an umbrella! But, I didn't *want* to go outside ... and then to a store ... and then to get out in the rain ... and go into the store ... and then come out in the rain again ... and ... I just *didn't want to!*

Earlier in the week, Joe and I had dinner at a Chinese restaurant. An acquaintance from years ago was having dinner. I stopped to chat for a few minutes and she told me that her cancer had returned. I listened and tried to be encouraging. A daughter of hers would soon be delivering twins ... I assured her that grandbabies are amazing healers.

Something inside of me was telling me to get an umbrella to her ... to tell her that she is being watched over and protected. Looking out at the rain, I was still trying to convince myself to hibernate. But this pull inside of me was nagging like my mom used to. It just kept after me and after me until I finally relented and drove to Wal Mart. What did I need? Nothing! Not one single thing except an umbrella!

I stood in the accessories department looking at umbrellas, wondering which one to buy. 'Well, I'll just go with my feelings I guess!' This whole escapade has been just a feeling anyway. Burgundy and Forest Green stripes – looked good to me. One item with me as I ran in the rain back to the van ... an umbrella.

The nagging still did not stop. At this point, I was

actually talking out loud to myself as I was driving. I was telling myself to just mail it to her – don't try to locate her. After all, that's what the lady in the story did – she mailed the umbrellas. The odds of finding this woman were slim ... this lady works at the hospital – I have no idea which of the three shifts she works, no idea which department. The hospital parking lot was packed full. Visitors were driving back and forth through the lot waiting for departing vehicles. Well, I had had enough ... I'm going home ... I will send it to her in the mail, just like the lady in the story. I was leaving ... I had given it my best shot ... and then ... there ... right there ... in the middle of the day ... walking to her car in the rain ... was the woman that I bought the umbrella for. I shook my head in disbelief, muttering 'unbelievable' out loud several times.

She was running in the rain and quickly hopped into her car. I pulled up behind her vehicle blocking her in the parking stall. I found myself wondering how I was going to explain this. To explain *why* I was tracking her down in a parking lot to give her an umbrella.

She got out of her car and asked, "Cathy, what are you doing here?" I looked her straight in the eye and said, "I DON'T KNOW WHAT I'M DOING HERE." I explained about the story, the lady, the umbrellas, the message that you will be protected and this umbrella will assist you with the afflictions of life ... I told her all of this as we hugged and talked ... standing in the rain.

She explained that it was not time for a shift change. She was leaving early – her daughter had just delivered twin

60

girls – both healthy. I just *happened* to be driving through an overflowing hospital parking lot at the *exact time* she *happened* to be leaving to see the babies ... too spooky!

 I had executed my task and drove home in the rain.

So much for casual reading.

Travis' Christmas Wisdom

Little Travis sat looking up at the 10-foot tall Christmas tree.

I know it was ten feet tall because that's how high the ceiling is. The only reason the tree fits in the house at all is due to the fact that a foot of tree had been cut off the bottom. I know ... I know ... I went overboard on the size of the evergreen – it's hard to judge the size of a tree when you're in the woods and there's no ceiling.

Travis is my first arrival each day for daycare. The house is peaceful and quiet. Each morning I turn the Christmas lights on and get water for the tree. The first week the tree took several quarts of water a day. Every morning Travis sits next to this massive pine looking up.

I was watering the tree one morning when Travis warned, "Cathy, you better stop waterin' that tree." His tone was serious and admonishing. "If you don't stop waterin' that tree … it's *not* going to fit back in the box!"

To Tracy

A thought provoking, insightful story has become my Christmas trademark ... instead of an annual family update I like to send a real life account ... something penetrating that reaches inside to touch the heart. I was especially interested in the reactions to *this year's* story because it's part of a book of stories that contain life lessons ... not just *any* book ... *my* book.

In past years people commented all through the holidays about the message in that years' story ... and this year NO ONE ... not one single person. I rationalized ... after all, I had sent the story out only a few days before Christmas. Friends probably didn't even read it yet! No matter what I told myself, the truth was, I was discouraged. My journal entry on Christmas eve is a pep talk to myself ...

I wrote:

"If the Christmas story needs to be rewritten, then it needs to be rewritten, that's all! Don't let it cast a shadow over the rest of your stories … don't quit! … everything's worth a shot!!"

The personal pep rally didn't' work. I wanted to quit … planned to quit … I was so disheartened.

What happens when you're feeling demoralized? Does your body send out a radar signal asking for help?

It was nearly 10:00 PM Christmas Night when the phone rang. And there it was … my gift … more than I could have ever asked for … a friend through the years calling to say that this years' Christmas story was outstanding! That every story through the years had been good, but this one … this one is 'exceptionally poignant'.

When something happens at just the time that you need it most … when it appears to be by chance — is it merely coincidence? … or is it a connection to the universe? … a connection to God? … a connection to humanity?

Did he call to tell me that I have a task … a purpose to be accomplished? That's not what he said … but I know that's why he called.

Thank you my friend ………

The Stupid Stick

Did I get hit over the head with a stupid stick or what?

I pride myself in being a person with a positive outlook. I see the good in other people most of the time.

For the past six weeks, I have been trying to have a conversation with one of my sons. A touchy matter ... an issue of pride ... and a serious case of the dreaded disease known as the GenX financial mentality. The issues needed to be faced. My son ... obviously ... did not want to discuss the topic. After weeks of attempting to speak with him I had become exasperated.

I was geographically too far away to be able to just take him by the arm and say, "Hey you! Sit your butt down right here, because I have some things I want to talk about." My calls went unanswered for weeks.

Last night, I realized that I wasn't focusing on the positive … I needed to change my thinking. I called my sons' cell phone and left this message: "I want you to know how much I love you … and how much I miss you … and I can't wait to see you again!"

Three minutes later my son returned my call.

Little Big Man

(Tom, Rob, John Age 17,19,21)

A week on a cruise ship in the Caribbean ... three nearly adult sons ... and Spring Break. What a combination!

The Piano Bar was just one of the late night hot spots that was rockin' all night long on the cruise ship. Piano keys covered with heavy layers of polyurethane formed the circular bar. In the center of the circle was a piano and the piano man. He was a lively character – with jokes and songs ... saving the loudest, rowdy songs for late in the evening.

One other guest on the ship, who would sing occasionally, was a somewhat shy and very large black man. When the portable microphone was in his hands ... when he opened his mouth to sing ... everyone waited ... what came out was sweet and mellow. If his personality could be put into music ... it was the feel of his soul coming out. The boys would stand on both sides of him rubbing the short curly hair on his head or they would have an arm thrown over his massive shoulders with heads tipped together and voices bellowing in song.

Every morning the boys would tell us about their adventures – the things that happened after Joe and I could no longer stay on our feet. What we heard about the man was "Wow! What a cool guy … a great voice … so much fun…" The list went on.

With the piano man at full throttle one night, I waved to my sons … they knew … I needed sleep. As I was leaving I saw this massive man in the hall outside the piano bar. I took the opportunity to ask him about his musical background. Did he work with music? " No" he said "I coach a little football but I haven't done anything with music since high school." We chatted for few minutes until my sons saw him … the beckoning from this college age group continued until our conversation was over by default … he *had* to go and sing!

The following evening after dinner the boys saw their new singing comrade … there were high-fives and hellos … laying out their evening entertainment schedule … the boys were trying to convince him to join them once again with the Piano Man. Tommy's face changed as he looked down for a moment … his tone changed to one of disbelief as he asked, "Is that a Superbowl ring?" The quiet man nodded and held out his other hand for the boys to see. "Uh huh, and this is my Hall of Fame ring." At that point I simply stepped back to watch. The excitement, the disbelief, the questions ... the poor man!!! Would he be able to hold up under the pressure of these three young men whose father has taught them there are two seasons in a year ... football and baseball.

I'm glad we didn't know about the Miami Dolphins. I'm glad we didn't know about the undefeated season. It gave us a chance to see beyond the football profession to the *other* greatness inside. He let the boys know, that fun is fun ... that people are people ... and that 'we're all in the mood for a melody...'

Larry Little ... the man who sings from his soul.

A Wellstone Memorial

Senator Paul Wellstone, his wife Sheila and daughter Marcia died together yesterday in an airplane accident.

The news reports continued to repeat the only bits of information that are available from this remote part of the state in Minnesota. An unusual situation for the press ... a terrain difficult enough to keep even reporters away. The only television footage we've seen of the location was filmed from the air.

Public radio spent days with the caller lines open. Hour after hour is filled with stories of nobility – honorable choices. The entire state is mourning together.

Why are personal values not a part of a campaign? Why are these pieces of the puzzle left to be found after the game is over?

I feel cheated ... robbed of a chance to meet a great man! I didn't know that he used his heart as his center of operation.

Had I known then ... what I know now, he would have been my hero ... not necessarily my political hero ... but my 'one person can make a difference' hero. He would have been my 'you can be political and let your heart be your guide' hero. My 'you can have your wife be your lover forever' hero.

I grieve for my loss ...   I didn't know enough to admire him until he was gone.

A woman caller said her family had always been supporters. When he visited her high school years ago, she said to the senator, "Mr. Wellstone, I want you to know that you're my hero." He replied gratefully, "What a wonderful thing to say ... Thank you." This caller motivated me to write a letter that was long overdue ... to my hero.

Sheila and Paul Wellstone were on a military base on the East Coast, when a female private approached Sheila explaining that she was a Minnesota admirer of the senator. Sheila insisted that she come to say hello to her husband. The private was reluctant, as Mr. Wellstone was talking with a corporal – but Sheila insisted ... Paul Wellstone was thrilled to talk with her – he made her feel important ... because she *was* important to him.

Another caller on the radio told that she was a campaign

worker who ushered Wellstone to his house with suitcases in hand from the airport one day. They were involved in a political conversation when they reached the Wellstone doorstep. The senator politely invited her to finish the conversation *the next day*. Sheila was not home. In that case he would not be inviting her inside. Honorable and smart.

The stories abounded until I could hear no more. There is no more room on my face for tears. It is almost too difficult to listen ... to hear the good things he had done and to know he is gone.

If we had a law that confined candidates to only talking about themselves ... maybe we would see the 'real' candidate ... the whole person ... their values ... their qualities. Minnesota is a good place to start.

Minnesota :   the home of hope.
               the home of optimistic people.
               the home of honorable people.
               the home of Paul & Sheila Wellstone.

My Hero

To: The President and Mrs. Carter

From: Cathy in Minnesota

Yesterday Senator Paul Wellstone died here in Minnesota.

Today I was listening to MPR while I was driving. Callers from all over the state were talking about the death of Paul Wellstone.

A young woman told of a day, years ago, when she had met Paul Wellstone at her high school. She and her family had been long time supporters ... and so she approached him and said "Mr. Wellstone, I want you to know that you're my hero." And his response, "What a wonderful thing to say! Thank you."

As I continued driving, the conversation inside my head went something like this. "I bet she's really glad she said it out loud to Mr. Wellstone. But me? My hero is so well known and highly regarded, that certainly one more person saying it, would make no difference." And then the other side of my head said, "Ya, but what about doing it for yourself? Because it needs to be said, whether anyone is there to hear it at all."

Mr. Carter you are my hero and here are the reasons why:
(In no particular order)

1) Because you choose to live a simple life with good friends.

2) Because you were wise enough to tell your friends and neighbors ahead of time, to not let Plains become commercial because of you. You kept their foundation safe.

3) Because you do things with your influence, that literally, not one other person on Earth could accomplish. You are part of a group-of-one who chose to take the noble path.

4) Because you understand that all of the accomplishment in the world (Nobel Peace Prize) are nothing without Rosalynn.

5) Because you had Rosalynn at high level meetings,

understanding that her perspective was valuable - and that you compliment one another.
The list goes on and on ...

I've enjoyed reading your books and lots of other writings about your life. In one book you said as a boy, you boiled peanuts to sell. (My husband Joe and I love boiled peanuts – we offer them to our friends here in MN but so far ... we don't have to share them with anyone except each other.)

Even though we live in Minnesota, my dad grew peanuts one summer when I was a little girl. We got quite a nice crop too! Well, my dad passed away this last year. And so, this summer I found myself planting peanuts ... in thick black rich soil, in a low area that holds the water ... in spite of the odds, I planted peanuts. As they grew, I just tried really hard to have the feeling of my dad back, just for a minute.

The peanuts? Oh yes ... it was a bumper crop ... at least a quart jar full!! We boiled them and ate them before they had time to cool at all. Besides the quart jar of peanuts, the plants yielded warm and comforting memories of my dad.

The world is a much better place because of the two of you.

Wishing you all good things ...   *Cathy*

A month after I mailed this letter, I casually mentioned to Joe, my husband, that I had finally written to my hero.

Another month later, on a Saturday, I told Joe that I was going to town to work on my computer for a few hours. I returned home in the cold about four hours later – taking off boots, snow pants, gloves etc. Joe commented that I had been gone such a long time … curious comment … since I had told him where I would be … and then once again he commented on the number of hours I had been gone … hmmm, not sure what that's all about.

As I stepped into the kitchen Joe was holding at arms length an envelope in front of my face. When I backed up so my eyes could focus … the return address was from the Carter Center.

I'm not sure what I expected to find inside the envelope but certainly not what was actually there. Inside was a hand written note, thanking me for the beautiful letter … signed *Jimmy C.*

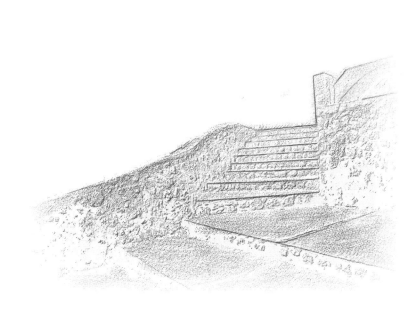

Young Legislation

You can always tell when a child is repeating something that's not their own thought, but that of a grown-up ...

It was an 80 degree day in mid-May - the kind of day that makes every seven-year-old school kid impatient for summer vacation. Cody was a boy, big for his age, just waiting to grow into his hands, like a puppy waiting to grow into its paws. Cody had an overly thick head of hair with a cowlick on his forehead that sat neatly above his big brown eyes.

On this particular 80-degree day Cody informed me "they oughta cancel school ... it's so nice out ... my dad says 'it oughta be a law, that nobody works if it's over 80 degrees in Minnesota!"

Smart dad ... smart kid.

Unspoken

The E-mail was from a 'bride-to-be'. She was a little nervous ... she didn't know why. Getting married really doesn't change anything. Right? Since they had been living together for years, everything would stay the same. Right? She wanted to know why she was feeling skittish.

I clicked on 'reply to author' and wrote:

My dear girl, without a doubt, you *should* be nervous and excited. Getting married *will change everything!*

Your love and friendship will become deeper than you ever imagined. Marriage sets in motion two people pulling in the same direction. It is a comradeship.

This man will become a husband and life together will be beautiful, not perfect, but beautiful.

There will be unspoken moments in bed, not always for sex ... a little foot searching for someone else's leg – an unspoken transfer of love. Without a word gigantic hands are pulling a small feminine body to his side of the bed. One touch can take your breath away.

There will be times when you go to bed, he will be reading. Without looking up from his reading he will lift his arm for you to lay on his shoulder. It is second nature now. There is comfort in the unspoken.

There will be times when words cannot describe the intimacy you share. How can you put into words something so private? An unspoken knowing ... that two people are meant to be together.

How sad it is when lovers who could have been the 'romance of the ages' part – not because love didn't exist at one time – but because love wasn't tended and cared for ... the unspoken needs care.

And so my friend, you have cause to be nervous. Something wonderful is about to start growing. You are going to love and be loved at a level deeper than words.

My Scarlett O'Hara Day

It was a beautiful day for a wedding. On this gorgeous, sunny, 90-degree day, I was pretending to be Scarlet O'Hara. In a nearly floor length bright yellow sundress with matching sandals I was strolling across the yard this perfectly peaceful day. Why Scarlett O'Hara? Because the dress made me feel pretty but the weathered hands and garden dirt under my fingernails was a dead give away. Nothing could change the mood of this day.

The bride *used* to be little ... and she used to be mine. Well ... at least part mine. Her mom and dad shared her with me while they were working. A little girl so delightful that getting paid to care for her was a crime.

I returned home after the wedding with thoughts of fairy tales still dancing in my head. Joe was stomping across the yard and into the house. I didn't know *what* was wrong, but I certainly knew enough to stay out of the way! He crossed in front of me through the doorway without saying a word. Must be something very wrong with the project he's working on.

The phone rang … it was Rob. Casually I said "Hey Rob! How ya doin?" Without greeting me, his serious voice said, "Have you talked to Joe yet?" No I had not talked to Joe … not with the mood he appeared to be in … oh no! … the realization struck me … Joe's mood was directly related to this 23-year-old on the other end of the phone line … who happened to be in jail.

Jail: an unfamiliar place. What street is it on anyway? My yellow dress with the matching sandals didn't seem appropriate as I walked into the Law Enforcement Center. But *what is* appropriate for an occasion like this? I have to ask a fashion consultant some day.

Expired license tabs … no *proof* of insurance … a previous count of no proof of insurance … $400 cash needed for bail. Rob's past year had been an extended period of partying and irresponsibility. I wasn't so sure I was going to bail him out. As the debate in my head continued Rick – the police captain – came out to the lobby to talk with me … I was grateful … if I had to talk to one more person through a two-inch hole, I was going to become a criminal myself.

The police captain said to me in a tone of appeal, "Cathy … he's a good kid. He was only a hair over the speed limit – I'm not even giving him a ticket! You need to bail him out." GREAT! A police captain is standing here pleading my sons' case – telling me that I need to get my..upstanding..son..out..of..jail. Is there an oxymoron in here somewhere?

Where do you find $400 cash (The Law Enforcement Center won't accept a check, not even from a non-criminal. Go figure!) on a Saturday afternoon? With some creativity I arrived back with the cash. The desk officer told me it would be at least an hour to finish paperwork.

An hour later Rob called my cell phone. He was out of jail and profusely appreciative. I wanted to talk to him face to face. I wanted him to come home with me to the farm. I could tell that he was hedging. The 23-year-old voice said "Well … uh … we have to be getting on the road … to St. Cloud soon … for my friends' bachelor party tonight!"

It was rage – pure and simple – that took over my entire being. I had paid $400 and spent a beautiful afternoon at jail … all, so that my son, who neglected to pay for necessities … could go to a bachelor party out of town! What a good mom! The party-goers of the world would nominate me for the Mother of the Year Award, all right!

As Rob and I arrived home Joe was back to working on the foundation for his shed. Me? I was still in my pretty yellow dress, which was *definitely not* the correct apparel for the occasion. My fairy tale day was fading fast. Once I was in 'home clothes' the discussion began.

Rob was saying that he absolutely *had* to go to this party, he had been planning it for six weeks! Planning a party for six weeks and unable to plan for license tabs and put an insurance card in his car? "I like my party life!" he insisted. Locking eyeballs I told him that he *did not* like his lifestyle – he just simply didn't know how to get himself out of it! The financial mess had overwhelmed him into inaction.

The conversation ball kept getting batted back and forth – Joe being a much superior parent that day, than I was.

It took me a couple of days to gather my thoughts and discuss them with Rob. I told him everything – every frustration I'd felt, from his financial woes to his crummy attitude. He had stepped over the line – the line of reason and common sense.

At the time, my Scarlett O'Hara day was a day from hell … but I wouldn't trade it for all the fairy tale times in the world because my Scarlett O'Hara Day became Rob's Decision Day.

The day Rob decided to take the blinders off … decided to step out of the rut … get back on the road. The road behind him is disappearing with every step, while a new path is rolling out ahead. I help him if he asks … but it's his road … his journey … now he is the explorer of his own path.

My Scarlett O'Hara Day was one of the best days from hell I've ever had.

One Gold Ring

An early morning sleepy glance into the mirror and I discover that I had been laying on something in bed. It left an imprint of a perfect circle in the skin on my shoulder. Now what in the world was it from? There were no buttons that could have caused it. I was thinking about it while I was waking up in the shower.

It wasn't until later that I realize that the impression is from my mom and dad's wedding ring that hangs from a gold chain around my neck. It wasn't really mom's wedding band – it was really 'their' ring – she wore it for the two of them. Dad's gigantic fingers were never made for such things. And so this ring was worn for both of them – worn smooth for almost half a century.

Mom lost weight during dad's illness. The gold band that was once a perfect fit was dangerously large.

Of course, we had taken mom to the jewelry store to have it sized … but they couldn't make the needed adjustments at that very moment while mom waited. To leave the ring there … even for a day … would have been unthinkable. No, if they couldn't do it immediately, then it would be put off until another day. But we knew it would never get done.

She wore it dangling on a tarnished tin chain until my sister replaced the chain with a gold link necklace. Now the old ring, worn and polished by time … love … work … and life, was on a necklace around mom's neck.

After dad and mom were both gone, one sister got mom's graduation ring … another had her old diamond ring and so, by default, I ended up taking this item home. I planned to set the chain and ring in a box – a memento to look at once or twice a year during times of reorganization. I planned that at those times I would see the ring and remember.

Often in my life I casually make choices that seem incredibly innocent. Minor decisions that are not particularly significant. So too, this day of carefully adding mom's ring to my collection of inexpensive adornments, seemed casual and without significance.

I didn't know … couldn't see ahead. It was a day of getting final notes and outlines and handouts ready for an out-of-town presentation. My mom and dad … my cheering section … my number one fans … were gone. Going to present at a conference or workshop without 'do a good job' and 'be careful' from these two people was just as unthinkable to me ... as was my mom leaving her wedding ring in the care of a stranger. What if the class didn't go well? Who would I tell? Who would care? Feeling all alone ... no soft place to fall if I fail ... no joyful celebration if I succeed.

And then ... I remembered it! The ring! Get the ring! To my amazement there was great comfort in wearing the chain with the ring around my neck. There, hanging above my heart, was a small piece of my mom and dad – a security blanket – tucked away just under the surface of my strength and confidence. The day I put the ring in my jewelry box, I couldn't foresee how much I would treasure the gold chain with the worn gold band on it.

The ring is becoming a part of me ... I wonder if I will ever take it off again.

Margaritaville

Heading for fun ... sun ... white sand beaches – not! The beaches were there all right ... but the fun and sun were missing. Myrtle Beach, North Carolina: A perfect place to meet good friends ... to build sandcastles.

Our first evening at the ocean was spent reuniting with old friends. Of course, all of us were hoping the sun would be out in the morning.

The next morning we woke up to rain ... my energy that day was used for hiding my disappointment. Pouring rain kept us either in a car or in the trailer or in stores.

Waking up the second morning with rain still pouring down had pushed me to my limit! We hadn't come all this way to sit in the rain! No way! Joe and I were laying in bed listening to the rain on the roof. I said "Honey ...

think about this. How about we go to a restaurant that has cable TV ... and see *which way* we have to go to find sun ... and let's pack up!" He thought about it a second ... we brought the idea up to our friends ... we had a quick legislative committee meeting. The proposal passed unanimously. With suitcases stowed in the back the four of us set out on a great adventure for the discovery of sunshine. The television said south was the way to go.

Half the fun was not knowing where we would eventually end up. The further we drove south, the warmer the weather got and the more sun was shining – we were singing along to the radio and chatting all the way. Our swimsuits just might see the light of day after all.

Ah yes, here it comes – the windows down and hot air surrounding us. Sticking his arm out the window and adoring the sun, our driver yelled over the sound of hot air streaming through the car – "Is this warm enough yet Cathy!?! Can you hear Jimmy Buffet singing 'Margaritaville'?"

We parked and walked just a few feet to the white sand beach, not believing that two hours earlier there was not a hint of sun to be found. We took our shoes off to walk along the beach ... a huge pier was ahead ... massive ... compared to docks on Minnesota lakes ... this thing looked like King Kong. You could actually walk *under* the pier along the beach.

When we came out the other side ... a vision loomed off in the distance. At that moment I knew ... I knew absolutely for certain that we had discovered paradise. White sand beaches, 92 degrees in the sun and off on the horizon is ... a Holiday Inn. Ah! ...... life is good!

Kindergarten

Best of friends - that's what we had become. With Tommy's big brothers gone to school, we had become partners. Working together all day long ... more than a mother/son ... we knew what each other was thinking. A pretty incredible friendship between a mother and a six-year-old.

The first day of kindergarten I tried to pretend that I was fine without Tommy, but I wasn't. It's the typical story where the little boy says assuringly, "You'll be O.K. mom. I'll be back right after school" Yup ... that was me.

I was consoled by the thought that Tommy had two older brothers to protect him. They left early on the first day of school to walk the two blocks to the transfer bus. The transfer bus would take them just seven blocks to Lincoln

Elementary School. There are no sidewalks on 13th Ave. to the school so the boys never walked to school, they took the transfer bus morning and afternoon.

Ten minutes after they set out on this first day of school, the boys came running back home! They thought they had missed the bus when actually they were too early for the bus. I sent the three of them running back to the bus stop. I called their dad and asked him to make sure that all three got to school.

Mid-morning a girlfriend called to see how Tommy's send off was on his first day of kindergarten. I told her that everything had gone quite well except for the glitch when they were scared they had missed the bus. As I was talking to her, I glanced out the window … and there … running down 13th avenue … was my little six-year-old. I blurted out "I gotta go!" and hung up without waiting for a response.

I stood on the front porch as I watched in disbelief … Tommy running down 13th Ave.! At Fillmore Street … he didn't look for traffic, just bolted across the street … bounded up the steps and jumped into my arms. He threw his arms around my neck, his legs around my waist and announced, "I quit school mom!" Still in my arms he leaned back slightly and said, "I … needed … you!" I didn't say it out loud, but he had done exactly what *I wanted to do.*

In a matter of seconds the phone was ringing. The principal … the teacher … the counselor … all in a tizzy that a student ... a kindergartner no less ... left school to go and get what he needed. Tommy and I had lunch together before his dad returned him to school. Tommy came home on the bus with his brothers. Thank goodness for every-other-day kindergarten. Tommy and I would have the next day at home together.

Two days later on Tommy's second day of school, he went off confidently. Mid-morning, I glanced out the window ... and there ... running down 13th avenue ... once again ... was my little six-year-old. This time there was a student teacher, in a dress & high heals, trailing fifteen feet behind ... trying to catch him! It wasn't even a contest!

This time Tommy looked before he ran across the street ... jumped into my arms ... leaned back slightly and said, "I ... needed ... you!"

The student teacher was seriously out of breath. I gave her the keys to my van so she could drive back to school. Once again Tommy and I had lunch together. Once again his dad returned him to school for the afternoon.

I'd like to tell you that Tommy came home again on his third day, but he didn't. There were many more days I *wished he had*, but Tommy never ran home from school again. Instead ... he grew up.

He's at college, now. Tommy continues to hear his own drummer. Still makes choices and decisions from a rock solid foundation ... knowing what he *needs* and *wants* and knowing the difference.

We are still best of friends ... still know what each other is thinking. But, now there are times ... when *I* run to *him* ... when I cry on his shoulder ... when I wrap my arms around his neck ... lean back just slightly ... and say, "I ... needed ... you!"

"Hey John, I Love You"

Three years of after-school basketball practices seemed fruitless until tonight ... this was the pay off. I was a proud mom, and could hardly sit still. The excitement and noise in the auditorium ... a hometown crowd ... this is what he had been working toward.

Stepping on the court that night, it was obvious that this was John's night. The entire first half, he was in the right place ... at the right time ... *every time!*

In the third quarter John was scrapping under the basket for a rebound ... jumped, came down hard ... and broke his foot.

Looking at the fresh cast on his foot with the crutches leaning against the table I questioned, " If you had known then ... what you know now ... would you have played the game?" Without a moment's hesitation the answer came, "Absolutely!" Basketball was John's high school passion. He had worked for it – he earned it. The broken foot was only a temporary inconvenience.

After three weeks on crutches the cast came off – the day arrived to get back in the game. I was running some errands for John in the afternoon and decided to stop at the high school to talk to him for a minute. The receptionist told me that John was in Physics – all the way down the hall, last room on the left.

I took a casual walk past science labs that were in progress – the classroom doors were open, with students coming and going. As I wandered down the long hallway there was a question floating through my head. What am I doing going to talk to John at school? This is uncomfortable ... definitely not the place for a mom. ... hadn't I made a decision to *never* look for one of my sons here? I had never broken my unwritten rule before.

Finally ... there it was ... last room on the left ... there's John.

As soon as the other students recognized me the whole class started heckling John. I thought they were giving him a hard time because his mother was at school ... not so ... apparently, the closer it got to graduation, the less time John spent in class. Today he was lucky ... his mom stopped on a day he happened to be in Physics.

John came to the doorway ... we talked for just a minute.

I wanted to get out FAST. I said good bye making sure to step back away from him. I didn't want to seem motherly.

I was rushing down the hallway – I was all the way down at the front doors when I heard John's voice yell, "HEY MOM!" I turned to look … there … hanging out the physics door was John. He hollered, "HEY MOM! I LOVE YOU!" Turning around I cupped my hands around my mouth and hollered back "Hey John, I love you!" I was stunned as I walked through the parking lot to my vehicle.

In that moment in time, I knew … I knew that he didn't care who heard it … didn't care if the whole world knew it. He loved me. In less than five seconds … in the most unlikely place … he gave to me a moment that will last a lifetime.

Father's Day Breakfast

The final paragraph of an E-mail note from my son John:

Well, mom that's all the news here except for Father's Day breakfast I guess. Well, Brady and I got up and went to his school. He showed me where he plays, and the things that he plays with. He also made me a paper tie that all of the dads had to wear. Then we sat down and had pancakes and fruit for breakfast, and we got our picture taken. We played for a little bit, and at about 8:30 I told him that I had to go to work. He started crying and telling me that he wanted me to stay and play with him. So I hugged him for a while, and then I set him down and he started crying again, so I started crying too, I'm sure the ladies there thought I must have been crazy. So anyway, I left for work and kept thinking about him asking me to stay and play with him, so I left work at about 2 so I could go get my son so that we could play

together. I went and got him during naptime, which at
your daycare was taboo, but they seemed not to be
bothered by it, and then we went home and went in the
pool, played baseball, and watched TV together. That was
our father/son bonding day and it was a lot of fun. When
we were in the pool after I picked him up, I gave him a
hug and told him "Brady John, you are my favorite son",
and he said, " thanks, you're my favorite dad" That's my
story and I'm stickin' to it.

I love you. Love John

A Summer Storm

I am someone's security. It may seem like a strange thought, that there are three people in the world who, as long as I'm living, look to me for a sense of refuge ... in the best times and the worst times ... I am their rock. I am the one they turn to ... do I want to be their rock? Yes, I do. I planned it that way. I have listened to them ... cheered for them ... cried for them ... and protected them. I consider my position an honor and a weighty responsibility.

Last week one night Tommy and four of his friends decided to go to a dance club about 45 miles from home. I rarely ever question their destination — this seventeen-year-old is responsible and wise. That particular night however, my intuition was telling me something was wrong. I kept battling inside myself, not able to come up with any logical reason for them to not go to the dance.

The weather had been hot and heavy throughout the day with storms rolling in as the afternoon crept by. As they were leaving they were assuring me that the storm was passing. The weather radar, did indeed, seem to show that the worst of the storm was gone. Still all of my senses told me to not let them go. I had no logical concrete evidence to use for my case. They left at 9:30 P.M.

At 11:00 P.M. the phone rang. A recording asked me if I would accept charges for a collect call from Tommy. The voice on the other end was scared and strained. He said they were only a few miles from home when it became obvious that this storm was bigger and stronger than anyone had anticipated. They turned around in the fierceness of weather that Minnesota is noted for. The heavy rains were forcing cars to pull over and semi trailer trucks were in the median. When he told me about trucks passing and throwing water up ... leaving them blinded ... I could tell he was shaken.

They made their way to the wayside rest area just a few miles outside of town. The storm had taken the power down at the rest area. A lone custodian with a flashlight sat in the dark on a bench. One other traveler, a storm-chaser, was angry because the batteries for his video camera went dead. Using a cigarette lighter to see the numbers it was at this point, that Tom called home. His shaky voice said 'Am I ever glad to hear your voice!'

What did he need? Reassurance and support. He described the storm to me—told me that they were safe. We talked for several minutes until he calmed slightly.

In his 17-year-old wisdom he said to me, "Whatever you do mom, don't try to come and get us! It is so bad out here!!" I assured him that I would not venture out especially since I knew he was safe.

No use trying to go to bed … there would be no sleep until the group returned. After midnight when they arrived, I realized just how serious the situation had been when Tommy's friends sincerely thanked him for getting them home alive.

How do moms know when their children are in danger? Where does it come from? As near as I can figure it has to do with being their refuge … how did I know that they should stay home? I don't know. But I know that the next time Tommy decided to go dancing, he came and told me they were going. But before they left that evening he asked me if I had any 'funny feelings' about the night … he wasn't joking when he asked.

A Precious Moment

I stand off to the side in the cool hospital room – the old man's surgery has been somewhat successful – at least he is not left in total blindness – after all, half sight is better than none at all.

The physician at the bedside is talking about choices. Is there care available at home or will a nursing home be needed? The doctor leaves them to themselves to ponder the options. The old man bellers "Ma!" and then again "Ma!" … and the gray-haired woman approaches the patient who has been moved to a chair in spite of intravenous tubes and monitors … this frail little woman sits on the edge of the bed next to the old man and he says in low confidential tones … "Ma, what do you think? Will we be OK at home?" For a moment the two heads of gray hair touch together – for that instant they are fused as one – and the woman replies in a soft assured tone, "Oh, I think we'll be OK." It is what the man wanted to hear – for they would go home together one more time.

Standing there in the room, I was an intruder in a conversation between two people who had labored together for nearly half a century - it was a privacy that was none of my business and yet I saw it … not just saw it, but captured it … and put it away in my heart … knowing that at a time forthcoming, I would need it to console my tears …

Yes, dad and mom died this year – dad in August and mom in November – They are gone and yet I know that I could not possibly ask for more – for I know full well, that if I asked … for one more conversation … one more dance … one more walk through the yard ... and one more apple pie … that one more of everything would still not be enough.

This year I have learned to stop and look deep into the eyes of people that love me.

This year I have learned that being there when someone needs me is the most valuable gift I can give to myself. I thought I was the giver, but I was the receiver.

The Hitchhiker

A forever ago my older brother, Jerry, was in the Navy, on a ship somewhere over seas. It was too far away for us to even imagine what kind of a world he was seeing. All us little kids knew, was that he was a very long way from home and that our mom and dad worried about him.

Around our home there was nothing but wide-open fields for miles and miles. I remember one particular summer evening as if it were yesterday. I can still feel the heat of the day being moved out by storm clouds rolling in.

I recall it so well, because we never saw strangers … not ever … and here was a real live one walking up our driveway. A young man, a hitchhiker, came walking up to the house while we kids stood and gawked at him coming to our door.

This man knew he was out in the middle of nowhere, he knew there was a storm coming, and he knew he needed to find shelter. He asked my dad if he could sleep in our barn for the night. He did not want to intrude on our home and family, yet he was in desperate need to find protection from the rain.

My dad loaded us all up in the car, the kids, my mom, and the hitchhiker. We drove the man to Paynesville where dad bought the stranger a room for the night along with a hot evening meal.

On the way home in the car that night I heard my dad say to my mom, "I just hope that if Jerry ever needs anything, that this kindness will be returned to Jerry." You see, my dad knew … he knew that what you send out is what you get back – only he didn't want it to come back to him – he wanted it to go to his son who was so far away.

Years later an uncle of mine asked me if I knew 'the rest of the story'? I was expecting Paul Harvey to step through a doorway.

He said several weeks after the incident my dad was telling a friend about it. The friend replied, saying it could have been a dangerous situation and maybe dad shouldn't have invited him into our car. My dad said, "You are absolutely right. I should have invited him into our *home*."

The Weaver

For Tim and Brenda family farming had lost its appeal … new careers were beckoning. And me? I was the lucky one. With both parents enrolling at the technical college, they needed care for their small girls.

Their three daughters had never been to a 'daycare' before. On a farm … in the country … you don't have daycare … you have *mom*. For baby Jessica, the change was troublesome … but for her mom and dad the change was devastating! I was concerned about *the parents'* anxiety level much more than their daughters'. Baby Jessica cried each morning when they dropped her off. As soon as mom and dad were out of sight, her smiles returned for the rest of the day—but convincing mom and dad of that was another matter entirely. I assured them that after about 15 days, the girls would make a complete adjustment.

As the weeks progressed … every morning was upsetting. For the first 14 days Jessica continued to scream every morning as her parents left for school.

On the morning of the 15th day, they brought Jessica in the house. I welcomed her saying, "Good Morning Jessica! Are you ready to play?" Without hesitation she reached for my arms. Jessica smiled and waved good-bye to her daddy.

Since that day, Jessica's father believes that I can walk on water. "How did you know it would be exactly 15 days? How could you know that?"

Love is sewn with tiny little threads that weave themselves into a tight mesh – creating a bond that will last a lifetime. Jessica and I had been weaving thread for 14 days … on the 15th day the bond was complete.

Jessica trusted me … and I fell in love with her.

Two Years and Two Months Old

Nap time on a warm sunny summer afternoon. This little grandbaby shouldn't be having a bottle anymore. *But, I am the* grandmother and if he wants a bottle of chocolate milk ... then he will have it. I gently lay him in his crib before removing his shoes. Even though it's a warm day, he wants to be covered with his fur blanket, the one he's become attached to since Christmas time. I hand him his bottle of chocolate milk. With the back of my hand, I caress his cheek and speak soothingly, "Oh Brady, grandma loves you soooooooooo much!" He slowly removes the bottle from his mouth ... turns his head toward my hand ... and kisses it. Without saying a word he returns to his bottle and nap. Life just doesn't get any better than this.

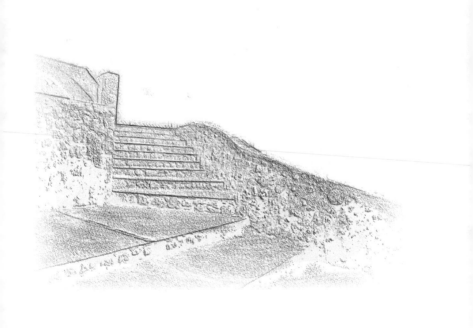

If You Miss Love, You Miss Life

I couldn't believe what I was watching from my bed. Across the hall from the bathroom, I watched my sister getting ready to leave for work. A quick brush of the teeth and a wash of the face – hair pulled back – old jeans and T-shirt ... walking out the door ... five minutes from the time she got out of bed. At straight up seven O'clock she was walking out the door. In my dreams! I would never be leaving the house like that ... but what does that say about me? Am I just used to seeing myself with make-up – I don't mind *not* wearing it – well, maybe I do.

So ... does that make her an infinitely more secure person than I am? I don't think so, but she is willing to just be herself.

In amazement, I watch Carol and the relationships she has with others – her willingness to be exactly what she is.

Maybe I envy that – people are attracted to Carol – rich people come to her home – a tiny cracker-box-of-a-home. They leave their mansions on a Saturday morning to have coffee at Carol's house. Why? Because she's the real article ... the real deal. No pretense ... what you see is what you get.

Carol is leaving the house early in the morning to go to the US attorney's office to clean. She cleans at the FBI offices on alternating days. Unless there's a Wonder Woman change over in the five minutes it take her to get there – I assume she arrives at work looking exactly the same as she did five minutes earlier when she left the house.

And these people – these people who work there – LOVE her! I mean, Carol has to start cleaning at one end of the offices – because she visits with the workers at the other end of the floor so much she can't get her work done! They are in suits and ties – she is in ... well, you know, I already told you. These people make no distinction – Carol is doing her job and they are doing theirs.

Richard was a client of Carol's. A stately gentleman I suspect from the talk I've heard through the years. Richard was a scholarly person – Vice President of a college - established the college's writing department. As a young retiree, he became an artist and did paintings. He had a gardener/frame-maker in his employ. Richard was looked upon as an icon of the city. As a matter of fact a festival that is named each year for someone notable, was one year named after him.

When she would be done cleaning at Richard's and ready to leave, Carol would holler to a distant part of the house … "I love you, Richard!" From somewhere in the house he would return 'I love you Carol – see you next week'!

Carol's other clients were much the same as Richard. The years have gone by with Carol working decades for the same families … creating a bond that goes beyond friendship … a bond that crosses into family.

Occasionally, Richard would ask Carol to make a hot dish for guests he had invited to dinner. Now, Richard generally just ordered dinner for himself, from restaurants … well … from restaurants that *don't deliver* … but they did deliver *to him.* It would amaze me when this gentleman with money and status would ask Carol to make a hot dish for his guests.

On one such Saturday, Carol arrived with the hot dish. As usual, she walked into the house without knocking. She shouted, "Hi Richard! It's me!". In the large house there came no answer. That was not unusual. Proceeding to uncover the dish and get it ready for the oven, she again called, "Hi, Richard!" No answer. Walking through the house she found the bathroom door ajar and the light on – not an unusual thing for a bachelor – Carol said he never shut the bathroom door when he had to go.

But today was different … today … Richard was lying on

the bathroom floor, having died there. It was Carol – an endeared trusted friend that found him there.

Several months later, a manila envelope arrived from an attorney. Richard's attorney ...

Inside was a cartoon style character drawing on parchment paper. In the picture there is a psychologist sitting in a chair with a notepad on his lap. On the couch is a patient lying down. Above the patient is a conversation bubble that says, *"You see doc, I've got this problem!!... It's an Ultimate Friends Syndrome! They keep doing kind and generous things for me! They have always been open and available to me – always! They gave me support when no one else did and backed me in my work and in the meantime they were fun to be with anywhere! So the question once more is, how do I thank them? Maybe saying I love them is enough."*

Of all the wealthy and influential people who were a part of Richard's life, the attorney had been directed to send out only four such manila envelopes after his death. If you miss love – you miss life.

Can you hire someone to love you? No, but for a hefty fee you can hire Carol to clean ... and love is a fringe benefit.

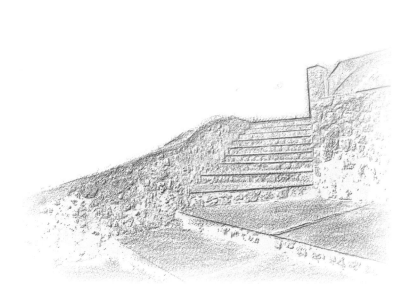

Daniel's Jewelry

(Location: Dominican Republic)

The shops at the outdoor 'mini-mall' were all numbered
... except for one ... the simple hand painted sign read
'Daniel's Jewelry'.

A tourist was asking the owner about his son as I browsed
... looking for hand strung jewelry at the ocean front
stores. The merchant replied that his son is eight now.
The visitor had been coming here for years. Looking at
me, the tourist pointed to a photo of a little boy. "This is
what his son looked like when I first started coming
here." I nodded, wanting to stay out of their reunion.

I found a necklace that was unique ... someone had been
creative ... it didn't look like all of the other pieces ... this
was what I had been looking for. Someone had taken all
the same supplies and tools but had created something
distinctive.

Then the tourist told me Daniel works to send his children to school – he is determined they get an education … I glanced at the shop owner. He was looking uncomfortable with the attention the tourist was bringing to him. Daniel shrugged his shoulders … in broken English he said, "it is all I have to give them."

I replied, "It is 'everything' that you are giving them."

The visitor paid for his items and went back to lounging on the beach.

I had chosen a necklace and bracelet by the time my husband entered the shop. Joe began negotiating with the owner. I know that dickering is how it's done in this country … but I wanted *this* necklace and I wanted to buy it from *this shopkeeper*. Joe started bargaining. He turned to me and asked if I was willing to pay $12 for both pieces. My answer was *supposed* to be 'no'. Then, I was *supposed* to start walking out of the shop with the owner chasing behind, offering a lower price. It was the game … it happens a thousand times a day in this 'shopping center'. Daniel waited for a response to the question.

Joe looked more than surprised when I quietly insisted, "I won't pay anything *less than* $12". Our eyes locked … a whole conversation took place in five seconds … he knew this was important to me. Taking cash out of his pocket Joe handed Daniel the currency.

Daniel said nothing ... took the money ... put my necklace and bracelet in a bag.

I was stepping out into the sun when Daniel stopped me. In my hand he placed earrings ... to match the necklace & bracelet. Without saying a word he smiled ... and went back to work.

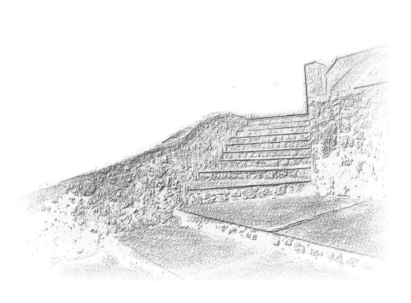

My Child's Child

Freeze a moment in time:

19 years, 2 months and 6 days after the birth of my first son John, I found myself in a hospital birthing room assisting the delivery of my child's child.

This 7-½ pound baby was born too early for the world. Two weeks of tubes ... medications ... incubators and ventilators.

Over two decades of childcare had not prepared me for the feelings that were ahead. Twenty years of touching, holding and carrying babies had created a permanent groove on my hip ... years of babies ... all kinds of babies ... big ones, little ones, fragile ones, blue eyed, brown eyed ... all unique and lovable. After all these hugs and kisses ... here lays a baby that I can't hold or touch. His eyes

and ears are covered with patches ... to close out the world and let him grow an extra two weeks.

Freeze a moment in time:

19 years, 2 months and 20 days after the birth of my first son John. I find myself in a rocking chair ... holding my child's child for the first time ... here he is in my arms.

In my heart I know that this child will never stop being the most magnificent product of raising John – the way things ought to be – a son having a son – my son now knowing for certain how much I love him ... because he knows how much he loves his own child.

Dalton

Dalton is a beautiful child – one of those kids that shoppers in a mall stop to stare at. Thick dark brown hair, swirl blue marble eyes and a contagious smile. Dalton is a storyteller – if the truth isn't interesting enough, he'll give you a full-blown story that will keep your attention.

One morning Dalton arrived at daycare with a scrape on his chin. Of course I asked a simple question expecting a not-so-simple answer from Dalton "What happened to your chin?" I asked. His eyes sparkled as the wheels of his mind began to turn. "Um...um, I was riding my bike, you know, on the cement in the driveway, and um... um... I ...I ...started to fall over and Um Um I ...I ... tried to catched myself and Um ... um, there was a rock in the way Um ... um ..."

I looked at his mother for an answer. She smiled a great smile. She explained, "He fell on the step going up to his brother's room!"

Dalton the storyteller!

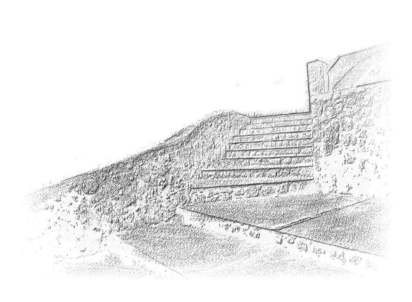

Grandchild of Mine

His first two weeks of life were spent in a hospital ... on a ventilator and drugs ... patches over his eyes and ears ... intervenes tubes ... monitors ... we watched as the doctors worked their miracles ... slowly ... the breathing came easy and comfortable...

As years went by and he grew, one of my favorite parts of daycare was after naptime ... picking him up from his crib. He would lay his sleepy head on my shoulder ... I savored the peaceful moments ... I knew that within ten minutes his energy level would be back to normal ... the placid time would be over. So I would hold and squeeze him ... looking off to the universe and the heavens. Sometimes I would say quietly "Oh ... I'm soooooo glad I have you."

Without thinking, the statement was occasionally

repeated as the months and years went by. I wasn't saying it to him ... not really saying it to anyone. I simply spoke out loud what my heart was feeling in silence. "Oh ... I'm *soooooooo* glad I have you."

In the blink of an eye this grandchild is almost too big for me to carry ... still I gently pick him up out of his crib. He lays his head on my shoulder. One day he leaned back sleepily saying softly "Oh ... I'm soooooooo glad *you have me!*"

Me too Brady ... me too.

Brown Baggin' It

So what kind of a professional schedules appointments at noon and skips lunch? I'll tell you what kind. The medical professionals that all tell you to eat three square meals a day! The same ones who never get eight hours of uninterrupted sleep ... never drink the eight glasses of water they should ... don't get the regular exercise they need ... all because of ... us ...

My appointment was scheduled for noon with a heart specialist. He was going to be reading all of his electronic tests and gadgets – looking at my health from the inside out. I did not like even *considering* that something might be wrong. All I wanted him to do was to tell me that I was fine ... strong ... healthy and I can be excused ... which is exactly what he did.

As he was leaving the room I handed him a brown paper

lunch sack filled with two turkey and cheese sandwiches and an extra-large Braeburn apple. I explained that I brought lunch for him. Knowing my appointment was scheduled at noon – certainly it meant he was skipping lunch.

The look on his face was stunned disbelief! "You brought me lunch?" When he realized I wasn't joking, the lunch *really was for him*; he accepted the bag saying, "Well, I *am* going to eat it – thank you very much!" My husband sat next to me shaking his head ... knowing that I have a purpose ... to make just one little part of my world a brighter place.

He was a doctor of the heart – I don't know why he was so surprised!

4 AM Wake-Up

"Well Cathy, is that you?" Even with his limited sight he saw me walk into the room. 'Yes dad.' I could see on his face he was pleased …. "What are you doing here already?" 'Oh, I don't know dad, I just woke up about 4:00 this morning!' I told the nurse I would finish feeding him breakfast.

Other than his comments during my surprise entrance, we sat in silence – he was in pain and nothing would take it away. And so we were quiet.

The doctor arrived with test results – it wasn't good. He asked me to step out into the hall with him.

He said that the tests were confirmed … it *is* leukemia … it *is* growing rapidly … and it will not be long … a month, maybe two. But I could tell by his eyes, that he was being generous.

Now comes the walk of a lifetime. When you turn to go back into the room. Knowing full well that the man in the bed is waiting for you ... to bring the verdict.

I lied right to his face ... I didn't have enough strength to pry the truth out of my mouth ... I could not repeat what the doctor just told me ... I couldn't believe it myself ... how could I possibly say it to my dad. I told dad he had two to three months to live. Quietly he said "hmm ... that's not very long."

I cried ... he knew I was crying. I tried to be quiet and not let it escalate to sobbing ... if I started, I knew there would be no stopping.

So I cried quietly and laid my head on his chest. It was bony, I could see the rib bones where the circle of the gown opening revealed his skin. Laying on his chest, I watched my tears drip onto that circle of skin. A big hand patted me. A hand that I never thought would ever be anything but strong and calloused from hard work. "Don't cry Cathy ... don't cry".

He wasn't wearing a hearing aid ... I sat close and spoke loudly. We talked about what mom should do, where she should live after dad wouldn't be there anymore. I told him that he needed to help mom make some good choices. I told him mom doesn't make good choices without him. He agreed.

He slept on and off. Soon, my brothers and sisters would be calling and arriving ... wanting to know what the days' tests revealed.

I needed to get out of the hospital for awhile. My brother was at work less than five minutes away, just across a four lane highway. I was about to leave the room when dad's protectiveness kicked into high gear. He blurted out "You be careful now, ya hear! Be damned careful!" He was dying ... and his concern was with me.

As I was leaving the room a nurse stepped inside the doorway. She commented, "I wasn't eavesdropping, but I couldn't help hearing your conversation" She said, "That was one of the most touching conversations I've ever heard".

Then I knew why I was awake at 4AM. I knew why I was at the hospital early. I was in the exact place ... at the exact time ... I was supposed to be.

Little Orphan Girls

I remember not wanting to tell anyone how I really felt. I was embarrassed to have these feelings at my age. I didn't think anyone would understand if I told them I felt like an orphan after losing my parents so close together.

I went to visit a friend who is nearing 70 years old. Until recently she was a daily companion … a visitor to *her* mother in a nursing home. Shortly after the death of my parents, her mother died as well. I remember thinking that certainly this woman in her late sixties, was ready to accept the loss of a mother who was past ninety years old.

I expressed my sympathy to her.

She got a far off look in her eyes and said quietly, "I guess
… you're never really ready to be an orphan … no matter
what age you are."

Though 20 years separate us … we are both little orphan
girls now.

The Other Side

I slip my hand inside his 'papa bear' sized hand. The fingernails have grown thick with age and a body once busy is now unmoving. Hour after hour ... day after day we hold hands. There is nothing to talk about ... nothing at all.

I say one more time " I love you" and one more time he replies, "I love you, too," then a pause and he adds, "I just can't tell you enough." The sentence goes unfinished, but I know the thought that drifts through his mind and heart. "I just can't tell you enough ... enough to last for all of the days that I won't be there. The accomplishments that I won't see ... the hands that I can't hold. How can he say 'I love you' to make it big enough and strong enough to last through the rest of my life?

Even though he can not respond I talk into his ear – telling him of the love his six children have for him. I remind him of the very special people who will soon be greeting him – people he has missed for a long time. Only moments before his last breath I lean over, kiss his cheek for the final time and say to him "I'll meet you on the other side dad OK? I'll meet you on the other side."

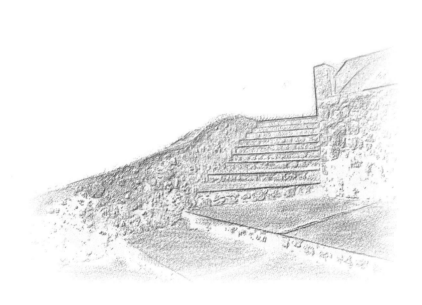

The Opal
(Cold Spring, MN)

Diamonds have never really interested me ... but I have opal rings to fit just about every finger. They've been collected and scrounged mostly from pawnshops through the years – a vacation activity.

Years ago jewelers (who wanted to sell diamonds) discouraged me from having an opal for a wedding ring. They discouraged an opal for being *any* kind of a daily wear ring ... and so I didn't buy one ... until one day I realized ... it was my money ... I had worked for it ... and if, I wanted to spend hard earned money on a ring with a stone that would disintegrate upon touching soap and water ... then that is exactly what I would do! Funny thing though, none of them disintegrated.

But for the majority of my life when someone would say 'the opal' it was not in reference to a ring or a delicate stone with rainbows spewing forth from its center.

Rather it was referring to a large hole-in-the-ground — a granite quarry — that, day by day, was getting bigger. I know all about it, because my dad put it there. Well ... not all by himself.

'The Opal' was right in the middle of the town where I went to high school. If I stayed after school for any kind of activity, my only transportation home was with dad. I walked from the high school to the granite quarry to wait for the workday to be over. Pieces of opalescent granite were being shipped all over the world for buildings ... dad was in charge of getting tons of rock safely out of the ground then loaded onto truck or train beds for shipment.

The men would go down into the hole using heavy metal grids and ladders for bridges & stairs that zigzagged their way to the bottom. At the very bottom was water. Water so far below ground level that the pool looked small from up above. In the winter, water that was destined for the pool below wouldn't quite make it. The water would begin its journey but ended up freezing in layers down the rock walls like a frozen waterfall. I remember marveling at the beauty of the wall of ice.

Explosives were used to loosen the rock walls. After a dynamite blast the quarry walls had to be inspected for unattached stone. One day as several of the workers were climbing down into the hole, a large piece of rock released itself from the wall and ended up in the water at the bottom. Tons of rock ... falling ... with no guy wires ...

one worker moved fast enough to get out of the rocks' path.

Unheard of in his time, dad stopped the machinery and ordered the men out of the quarry. He told management that the workers were not stepping into the hole until the walls were safe.

If I were there watching now, I would have hundreds of questions ... but back then it was nothing out of the ordinary to see a multi ton mass of stone being hoisted out of the ground, it was day to day activity.

The hole kept spreading as old homes and buildings were methodically torn down to accommodate the expansion. The time came when the hole could spread no further. No longer producing enough building stone to justify the machines and labor, the decision was made to fill it back up! I found myself not believing what I was hearing – fill it back up? A hole that has been quarried for decades and now someone casually decides to 'fill it back up'?

There were acres and acres of granite that had been quarried and stored for another time ... pieces that were considered junk because the color didn't flow the way the engineers had hoped. With this rock and stone from quarries all over the world the hole dad put in the ground was filled back up.

Town feels empty to me now. My dad is gone ... the hole in the ground is filled. I searched and searched for something to fill the hole dad left in my heart ... silly me ... it should have been obvious ... time filled it ... with an opal.

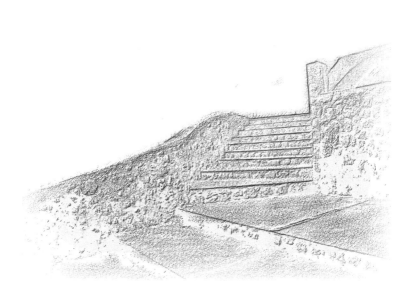

Sweet Sixteen

Tommy's 16th birthday started out the same as his older brothers' 16th birthdays had been ... a 9:00 AM driver's test. He passed it. By 9:45 he was gone – driving solo - *free* at last!

Tommy's friends who have not yet been 'freed' by a driver's license descended upon him. A car ... a driver's license ... what more could you ask for?

Stipulating that there was no out-of-town driving they left to pursue independence.

Hours drifted by on this late August day when my brand new, first day, sixteen-year-old came walking in the house. He said, "I need to talk to you" while his eyes were motioning to an empty room – and then more urgently he said again, "I *need* to talk to you!"

With the door closed behind us his words burst out like an erupting volcano. He had a friend in his car – they were talking – he wasn't paying attention to the road - it had rained several days previous - the shoulders on the roads were soft - going around a curve two tires got off the pavement - the soft shoulder pulled the car into a ditch full of mud. I interrupted, "Are you all right?" Yes, he assured me that he was O.K. but his *car! His car!* He took me to the window to show me his car in the driveway.

Dirt, muck, sand and gravel more than half the way up the body of the vehicle. They tried to get out of the ditch themselves, but only dug themselves in deeper. A man in a four-wheel drive vehicle came by ... stopped ... pulled them out of the ditch. Tommy offered the man every penny he had on him. The man refused saying, "Oh no ... I can't take any money ... I was sixteen once myself. "

So ... here he was ... home and safe.

Hosing the car down created so much sand on the concrete driveway it had to be shoveled into a container to be hauled away. Sand was jammed under the body and frame of the car. When Joe arrived (our family auto expert) to check for structural damage, he found the sand was pushed *into the tires*! With some balancing, aligning and clean-up, Tommy was back in his car again.

That night, in my heart, I thanked the man who pulled them out for teaching Tommy there are good people everywhere.

I thanked the universe for teaching Tommy a lesson and keeping him safe at the same time.

… and I thanked God for the privilege of helping Tommy grow.

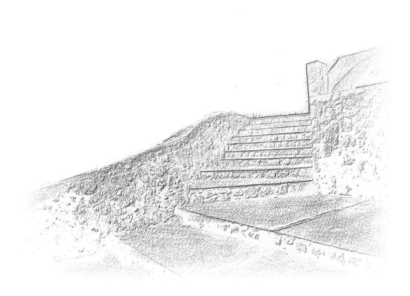

Big Gruff Man

He was a handsome enough man. But he had a stern looking face. He was someone that you certainly would *never* approach with a Midwestern 'hello' just in passing. A man that looks as if he worked hard at keeping his face straight, long and serious. This man was all business. His bedside manner was impersonal and factual.

The small town talk spoke of his lack of personality, lack of humor, lack of anything that made him appear human.

Then, one night I had the opportunity to watch this doctor when he didn't know that I was watching. This is how it happened:

My youngest son, Tommy, was about two years old when he ended up with a lung infection. This doctor's main emphasis was the care of children. Myself having three children born in a four-year period, this gruff individual was a fairly regular part of our life.

The decision was made to hospitalize Tommy and put him in an oxygen tent in pediatrics. Late afternoon I left Tommy at the hospital and went home to shower and eat. In the early evening, I went back to the hospital. When I arrived, the children in pediatrics had all been put to bed for the night – all of the room lights were out and just the hall lights were on. The hall lights shown softly through the observation window in Tommy's room, creating a nightlight affect inside the room. I pulled up a rocking chair and proceeded to sit there, watching Tommy breathe for the night.

It was about 3:00 AM when this physician went into the room across the hall. I sat there and watched as this impersonal man examined a newborn baby. His large hands ... ever so gently ... turned the baby on her side ... his hands checked the stomach area. He uncurled her tiny fingers, looked at the nails, and did the same with the toes. He checked charts. Then he stood back a few feet from the bassinet ... he crossed one arm and propped the other arm allowing his head to rest like 'the thinker'... and he stood there looking at the baby …….. and he stood there……….and stood there…….

Every so often he would shake his head as if to say 'what am I missing?' 'what is it that I'm not seeing?' This heartless man stood over this baby for nearly twenty minutes. Finally, he made some notes on her chart. Once again, the big hands moved the baby ever so gently back to her original position ... the baby never woke.

At that point in the night he came into Tommy's room. I scared the daylights out of him – he didn't know there was anybody sitting in there. I didn't know he would be keeping night watch with me.

Tommy was able to come home a couple days later.

After we were home I took a small piece of typing paper and a black magic marker. I folded the paper in half and on the front of the homemade card I wrote THANK YOU FOR TAKING CARE OF MY SON, and on the inside page AS IF HE WERE YOUR SON. Not much to it, just typing paper and a marker – popped into an envelope and sent it to the clinic.

Tommy had a follow up visit scheduled in ten days. So ten days later Tommy and I were at the clinic waiting in an exam room. When the doctor walked in, without hesitation he said "Thank you for the card". I started to say 'you're welcome' but he cut me off saying "No ... really ... thank you for the card!"

Well, Tommy is an adult now – and just as years and circumstances change us all – so too, the hard exterior of this man has fallen by the wayside. The man laughs, smiles, and tells jokes ... as well as being educated ... he is warm, gentle and concerned. I always give him a Midwestern 'HI' when we chance to run into each other.

One day, I finally got up the nerve to tell him about what I saw that night ... and the fact that I tell the story in public presentations ... but I quickly assured him that I had *never* used his name – only the story. "Use my name!!! Use my name!!!!" he joked and smiled.

From the moment I watched him stand over the baby ... I knew there was somebody else inside ... it just took a while ... for the real person with the heart to step forward.

Mr. Trooper

Dear Mr. Trooper,

I'm sure you don't remember me. I was on my way to St. Cloud with my elderly parents on June 28th, 2001 when I met you. It was a hot beautiful summer day in Stearns County. Since I went to high school in Cold Spring, I assumed that I knew the posted speed limit – I saw your car turn around in my rear view mirrors but it never occurred to me that *I* wasn't following the speed limit.

My dad, who was very sick, these past two years, only had half of his eyesight. He was sitting in the front passenger seat and wanted to know why I was pulling over. I said "Well ... because there's a highway patrol behind me with its lights on." My dad immediately grabbed for his seatbelt to buckle-up, (pretty sharp for a sick man huh?) but with his limited vision, he was unable to find the receptacle. You came to my window while dad was still trying to connect the mechanism. Your comment to him was, "You've got it backwards sir—you put the seatbelt *on* when you're driving and take it *off* when you stop."

Well, by this time I was totally chuckling inside myself!!!

While you went to check my driver's license, I got out of the van, went around to the sliding door and buckled in my 80-year-old mother.

When you returned my mom proceeded to shake her finger at you and tell you in a very motherly way, "I'll have you know, that when I was growing up, we *walked* wherever we needed to go." And your reply to her: "Ma'am, if you're *walking*, you don't *have* to wear a seatbelt."

Then you asked us what we were going to St. Cloud for – to visit friends? No, we were taking dad to chemotherapy at the hospital. You expressed your wishes for health and blessings to my dad. You made him smile ... you made him take his mind off his troubles for a few minutes ... you also took the time to tell my mom and dad about your grandfather who hit his head very lightly in a car and it caused him severe injury ... every word you spoke was done with the utmost of respect for the three of us.

Well, my dad passed away about six weeks ago now – I told the 'getting-pulled-over-story' at his memorial service at the Wenner Funeral Home – not far from where we met you.

Sir, you taught me a powerful lesson that day. I learned: You never know when *you* are the best part of someone else's day. We did blood tests & chemotherapy in St. Cloud that day and truly the bright spot of *our* day was *you*.

June 28th, 2001 *you* were the best part of our day. I cannot thank you enough.

Cathy Weber-Zunker

Santa's Day at School

(John 13, Rob 11, Tom 9)

As a parent, I was out-growing elementary school. It was hard for me. Elementary school was accepting of moms and dads coming and going. I was involved in my kids' lives even at school. But once John started middle school there was an unwritten rule that went into effect – moms don't go to school ... not at all ... not for any reason ... never ... ever!

It was nearly Christmas ... I really wanted to make some treats to take to school – I could go to the elementary school - the dilemma – of course, was that it's not cool for mom to go to junior high.

I called a girlfriend of mine to do a little brainstorming. She said she still had the Santa suit her husband used the previous year. I could borrow if I wanted a disguise. Hmmm ... A little bit of stuffing here and a pillow or two there … it just might work. It seemed like a good idea at the time.

The two of us figured out the best plan of action. I was going to get 'in-to' and 'out-of' the junior high school without anyone knowing it was me.

I called the principal and explained what I had in mind. He said, "Oh Cathy, this sounds like fun! Stop at the office when you get here and I'll go along to watch!"

By the time the afternoon arrived, there was heavy snow falling and the possibility of icy roads. Wearing my Santa gear I stopped at the office. The principal told me to go ahead by myself, that he had to make transportation arrangements.

I went strolling down the hallway readjusting pillows … pushing the beard up … pulling the hair down to nearly cover my eyes. With my sack on my back I was almost to John's classroom. Every few feet junior high students would stop me … looking at my eyes, to see if they could figure out who was inside.

After my stop & go walk down the hall, I finally stepped into John's classroom. Out of the corner of my eye I saw John sitting in a middle row, two seats from the back wall. Once I located him I made sure to not look his direction. The whole class sat and watched me, Santa, pass out candy and treats. The teacher played along beautifully, him doing all of the talking. The treats were passed out … I was tying my pack. I had done it! I threw the sack over my back, leaned back, took a deep breath, and in my lowest voice said "HO! HO! HO! AND A VERY MERRY CHRISTMAS!!!"

From the back of the room I heard my son John say, 'Huh! That's my mom!!!!!!'

I spoke not a word and went straight to my van...

Later John hooted, "I *knew* it was you as soon as I heard your voice!"

Together John and I went to the elementary school to Rob's class and then to Tommy's 3rd grade class. There, the rope that held my pillows and Santa pants up, let loose. The 3rd graders were in hysterics as the pants hit the floor.

Why do I do things like that?

I do things like that because I want my sons to know ... that in all of God's creation I was given the three most precious children in the world.

If we don't tell them now how special they are ... they *will* notice.

If we don't tell them now how special they are ... time will not stand still.

We have time in life for anything ... we don't have time for everything.

Shut It Off

Like a bunch of dingbats we were playing in the snow! It just happened. Three near teenage boys, a 105-pound dog, snow, snow tubes, and a long snow covered hill with a frozen pond at the bottom.

Here we all were, Joe and I, three sons, a dog and the light of a full moon. There's something magical and mystical about a full moon on a winter's night. It's like having God's approval to stay up past bedtime.

Each trip down the hill in the snow tube, went a little farther - as the packing process progressed, crunching the snow inch by inch, closer and closer to creating a freeway to the pond. When the direct path is finished we will be able to start at the top of the hill, proceed down to level ground, scoot across pondweeds at the perimeter, and continue all the way across the frozen pond. The ultimate in nature's entertainment.

Too bad for television – it just can't compete.

The Night I Knew

When I tell people my passion in life is public speaking they look at me quizzically ... like a dog with its head cocked and ears perked up. Before Joe and I were married I would tell him about my love for presenting. My passing comments about a possible future doing professional workshops went unnoticed, since children ... my very first love ... consumed the majority of my time.

So Joe thought nothing of it when I told him I was putting some materials together for a class on loss ... a support group specifically designed for recently divorced individuals. The subject was self-esteem and the presentation was to be 25 to 30 minutes.

It had been a long time since I had actually outlined and presented anything. I did not discuss the topic with Joe. I spent hours researching and organizing ... and loving every minute of it ... it was like slipping into a comfortable familiar pair of old slippers.

Joe and I went together to the small group meeting

Doing my homework paid off. The points had an easy logical flow that led to a lively and involved discussion afterwards. Small groups of friends stayed later to chat. When nearly everyone had gone, I gathered my materials and headed out the door, with Joe behind me.

When I stepped outside the building, I felt a masculine arm around my waist and another behind my knees. In a moment I was off the ground in the arms of this tall strong man who carried me to the vehicle. I was stunned ... but I was even more stunned when I realized why he had done it. The simple flow of information and my comfort at the podium overwhelmed him. "Wow!" he said, "You were incredible! You said you loved speech but *this was something!*" All the way home he showered me with praise and disbelief.

That was the night I knew ... I knew there was a message inside of me ... I knew I had to do something with this dream that was growing silently inside of me.

'Here's Lookin' At You Kid'

People-watching … guessing relationships … families reunited … little kids running to mommy or daddy's arms.

Air travel is my favorite spectator sport.

The performance is better than movies … way better than TV … better than any style of fiction that's available. The airport is REAL! A place where people pay good money to get in to watch this show.

At the age of 3 ½ my grandson (and his parents) moved 1,894.21 miles away … in that moment my entire attitude about air travel changed. It used to be something for vacations … now it's for survival.

✳◇✳◇✳◇✳◇✳

I waited my turn to 'deplane' while all the travelers were gathering carry-ons from the overheads. I knew that at the end of this walkway ... was Brady. We had made it ... we had both survived three *months* apart ... at a time in our lives when we had never spent three *days* apart.

Stepping off the plane in Tucson that first time ... I crouched down with arms spread wide ... nothing ... absolutely nothing ... could feel as good as holding him in my arms once more. Brady tucked his face into my throat. I kissed his cheeks until they could hold no more. We didn't let go for a long time.

As we walked away, his little hand in mine, there were travelers trying to hide their interest and curiosity and some trying to hide their tears. We were the show that day. We sucked them into our love...

When the missin' gets too hard. When my world needs the eyes of a child to keep perspective. That's when it's time to shop for airline tickets.

I knew when they moved to Tucson that this 'once-a-year' or 'once-every-other-year' visiting schedule some families talk about was obscenely inadequate. Actually it borders on the ridiculous. Non-stop flights – *two a day* - from Minneapolis to my grandson. I am sure that Northwest Airlines created the flight schedule to accommodate this lonely grandmother.

✽✧✽✧✽✧✽✧✽✧✽

It used to be touching to watch airport greetings & farewells. September 11th changed all that. That cozy boarding area to sit ... talk ... say goodbye is no longer a reality. The last glances or tears or smiles of love between the 'go-er' boarding the plane and the 'stay-er' who drives home alone ... the Casablanca style farewell is obsolete.

Ah yes, Casablanca ... if I close my eyes I can almost hear the roar of the plane ... feel the mist of the fog. A man in a suit with wide lapels walks to the aircraft. His wide brimmed hat is tipped to one side as he removes a lit cigarette from his mouth. His free hand just barely brushes across my chin. In one final parting moment he says quietly, 'Here's lookin' at you kid' and walks away into the fog. The intensity of airport farewells is the stuff that movies are made of ...

'Farewells' are said earlier now ... before security.

I made a solo visit to Tucson ... it was a 'Brady-fix' in other words. It was just John taking me to the airport for my return flight. I was trying to convince myself that this farewell would be easier without Brady being there. John lifted my suitcase to be checked while I got my boarding pass. At airport security I claimed a place in line before we said good-bye. Oh man, this is the tough part. My body sank into his hug. We both said the important things that were on our mind. He told me 'Thanks for comin' mom. I love you." I told him 'I love you, Johnny.

You are *so very* precious to me'. The embrace ended. Digging through my purse, I couldn't believe I was at the airport with no Kleenex.

I was juggling my purse ... book bag ... driver's license ... tickets – but I needed just one last look at this child-of-mine. He was already putting his sunglasses on, about to step onto the descending escalator. I couldn't let the chance pass, knowing that it would be months until I have him back in my arms. I hollered across the terminal "BYE JOHN!!" and gave him a nose-pressed-against-the-window' wave good-bye. He left the sunglasses on and waved once more.

As I turned around, the line that was in front of me was gone. Rushing to pick up my bag I apologized to the security official. "Oh my gosh, I'm sorry!" I said. He politely told me, 'Oh that's O.K.'. He checked the ticket and the license ... again compared the ticket and the license ... and then once again the ticket and the license. Finally I realized that he couldn't *see* the ticket and the license because of the tears in his eyes.

He was a part of our moment ... felt the emotions.
We sucked him into our love ...

Before September 11th

A woman with beautiful silver gray hair – laying in

190

perfectly soft waves was chatting lightly with a young man. He had books and a carry-on bag. He's (son) the 'go-er' – she's (mom) the 'stay-er'. When he was called for boarding, I had to look away. I didn't want to intrude on a moment that can only happen between a mother and son. The embrace lasted so long; I peeked to see if it was over yet. I cried when I saw them. They sucked me into their love …

Air travel … my favorite spectator sport.

"I Don't Care"

(Rob Son #2 19 years old)

After graduation Rob, moved to an apartment just six miles from home. I remember thinking to myself – 'Oh good, this is going to be so much easier than it was when John left for college two years previous – this is going to be a smooth transition, sort of easing into it. I'll be able to see him often – chat on the phone - convince myself that he's *not really* moving.

As the weeks went by Rob stopped at home occasionally, just long enough to pick up items he needed for his apartment. With a quick "I love you mom" he would be on his way out the door.

After a few weeks ... there were some realizations that began to set in ... things that hadn't occurred to me before.

Number one, was the realization that this son wasn't going to be coming home for the weekend ... not this weekend ... not any weekend. He wasn't going to be back in his own room ... in his own bed. There was no need to come home for the weekend when you live just six miles away! No need to come to the table for dinner. No need to hangout watching television ... no need for anything anymore ...

As these realizations crept in, I denied them. I kept rejecting the thoughts and putting them at the back of a dark closet in my mind ... shutting and locking the door. The closet was getting filled up.

I forced myself out of the house to stay busy ... made lists of things TO DO. I forced myself to go grocery shopping ... not think about it ... what was I going *to do* with all these feelings if I let them out?

Groceries to buy – enough to feed 10 little people for a week. This will keep me occupied, I thought. I went shopping and held back the emotions ... glancing at the lock on the closet door.

When the grocery cart was overflowing I went to the check out counter. A high school classmate of Rob's was checking groceries for me. "Did you see Rob?" she asked. Trying to hide my feelings, I said, "what do you mean?" She said, "Rob just walked into the store a minute ago, did you see him?" "No, I didn't" I said ... almost unable to speak. I didn't know what to do.

Finally, I said, "You know Angie, when Rob was growing up, we used to call him 'The Wanderer' because we always had to page him when the rest of us were ready to leave a store." Conspiringly, I asked her, "Why don't you page Robbie for me?" She looked around to see if any managers were close by and found it clear. Into her microphone she said. "Rob Weber to the courtesy counter please, Rob Weber to the courtesy counter please!"

I was still unloading groceries from my cart when Rob came around the corner. We both started laughing hysterically when he saw it was me paging him. He said, "It's been a long time since you've had me paged momma." We laughed together as he volunteered to start bagging my mountain of food.

After writing the check I moved to the end of the conveyor to help bag. Standing over a grocery bag, my long hair hanging down on both sides of my face, tears were dripping onto the packages. Without looking up I quietly said "I don't know why Robbie, but I've been missin' you *really bad*." It was at that moment he looked over and realized that behind the long hair, I was crying ... unable to hold the mass of emotions back any longer.

Right there ... at the check out counter ... this six foot four child-of-mine put his arms around me and let me cry into the softness of his winter jacket. When it was evident this wasn't going to stop soon, he stood up leaving my feet dangling, for what seemed like forever. Finally I whispered, "Maybe you should put me down Robbie, there are people lookin' at us." Staying solidly where he stood he spoke the three sweetest words I've ever heard. He said, "I don't care."

When the tears subsided ... I wiped my eyes and blew my nose. I left quietly with my cart full of bagged groceries and waved to Rob as he stood visiting with his classmate.

The next afternoon Rob appeared in my doorway with a smirk on his face – I looked at him and said, "I'm sorry Robbie! I didn't mean to cry!"

As we hugged he said, "You know ... it felt really good to be missed." After I left the store, his classmate, Angie, said it was one of the neatest things she'd ever seen.

Rob is like a batch of cookies that are absolutely perfect the first time. The rest of your life ... each time you make those cookies ... you try to make the magic happen again ... but they're never quite as good as the first time.

If I knew what ingredients produced this young man I would bottle them. But I can't for the life of me remember if it was a dash of perfection and a pinch of happiness or the other way around.

Tobacco, Matches and Toothpicks

It was everywhere! He was always pounding his pipe outside on the porch step or banging it on the edge of a glass ashtray. It would take two or three book matches each time he lit up ... so the ratio of tobacco to matches was about even.

Two or three puffs was all it took to satisfy him leaving a barely burned bowl of tobacco. Why didn't he just put less tobacco in the pipe? ... why didn't he reuse it? ... why didn't he let the pipe go out and then save it to relight the unburned tobacco? Still there were always ashtrays filled with cardboard book matches and unused tobacco. The habits of a lifetime.

And toothpicks ... oh, don't let me forget toothpicks! Toothpicks were just as ingrained as smoking. Front pocket on his blue denim work shirts always held a two or three day supply.

After dad died two of my sisters each took one of dad's pipes. They took them home to set them in a quiet place reserved for missing him.

Months later I drove his boat-of-a-car to town for repairs. My dad's car ... now it's mine ...

Driving down the highway, I noticed the open ashtray. There it sits, overflowing with unburned tobacco, book matches, and toothpicks. Just the way it always was ... so much like normal ... from when he was always there ...

At the repair shop I gave a specific instruction, "Don't let anybody empty that ashtray O.K.?"

I divided the tobacco, the matches, and the toothpicks into two crystal bowl shaped dishes with high sides. I carefully covered them with plastic wrap.

The sisters who took the pipes didn't know I had an item to make their quiet place complete. So here we are ... sisters together ... laughing at anything. When a tranquil moment arrived, I asked ... "By the way, who took dads pipes?"

My two sisters replied, "I took one" and then the other sister, "I took the other one". "Well in that case," I told them, "I have a gift for you." From behind my back I revealed the two crystal bowls of tobacco, matches, and toothpicks.

It took a moment for their eyes to focus ... another moment to realize the bowl was filled with a lifetime of memories. Imagine ... discarded pipe tobacco ... more valuable than gold to us ... a hint of our dad ... tobacco and matches and toothpicks.

'Another Forever': A Definition

Looking back I can't imagine a time when you were not a part of my life.

Looking ahead I can't imagine my future without you – so the way I look at is … I've loved you forever already and I'm looking forward to loving you for another forever.

There are only certain people who qualify for the 'another forever' category. They are the people who, since almost the first time I met them – I knew they would be a part of my puzzle. People, who like *themselves* enough … that they confidently hand out bits of their life perspective everywhere.

My favorite people are 'piece seekers'. Those who are excited to share their newest building block about LIFE. The person I share with becomes a part of my puzzle … I become a part of their puzzle ... we have changed the structure of each other's lives ... we will never be the same again.

Once a piece of the puzzle is in place ... it can never be removed ... in other words ... you will be in my heart for 'another forever'.

On saying 'I Love You'

Some people hoard their 'I love you's. I must admit I give mine out more freely since a brief incident one day made me stop and think.

I was leaving my chiropractor's office one afternoon, when Joyce, at the front desk, hollered after me, 'I love you! See ya later'.

Joyce is one of those people who, makes you feel better even without an adjustment. She and I have spent years building a friendship.

Hmmm ...... I thought. I went to the van and let it sink in. How did I feel about it? It was true ... we are close ... but it was in public ... and two women ... then as I drove away I realized that ... I liked it ... it was completely comfortable ... so why not say it out loud? There are other patients coming and going at their office ... no one seems to mind ... as a matter of fact they don't mind at all ...

Since that day we never part without our, "Hey, I love you ... can't wait to talk to you again" greetings. It made me look at my relationships – I took personal inventory to make sure I'm saying it ... out loud... without reservation. When I looked at my attitude toward saying 'I Love You' this is what I found.

First, I don't say it unless I mean it.

Second, I say it only to people with whom I would also use the ' forever' word - someone that I enjoy so much I can't imagine a time in my life without them. So when I tell someone that I love them - it means *just that and nothing more*.

Third, if I say it once ... then it applies to every day for the rest of time ... no matter what direction their life takes them and what direction my life takes me ... decades from now ... I will still tell them that I love them, because I do. It's that simple, I just want them to know that I like who they are ... always have ... always will.

And by the way ... I Love You.

Annie's Wisdom

Annie's daddy was in a hurry. Getting the children ready by himself, in addition to getting himself ready for work was an unfamiliar task.

Annie was sitting on the floor attempting to put on her own shoes. Daddy picked up a shoe, to help hurry the process along, and said "Annie, you've got the wrong shoe."

Sweetly, innocently she replied "No daddy, you've got the wrong foot."

Perspective: neatly packaged ... with a bow on top.

Check's in The Mail

Once upon a time ... a long long time ago ... when checks were returned to you in your bank statement. No statements were mailed out; you picked them up when you went to the bank to deposit your paycheck! The employees at the bank even knew who you were... and who your kids were ... and ... well ... everything about you.

During those years my dad and I had a game we played. Occasionally I would write a check to him – he would endorse it and below his scribbley, indecipherable signature he'd add a messy handwritten note that almost looked like – 'I Love You'. Weeks later, when I balanced my bank statement, the first thing I looked for was the check with the note. The next time I'd see him he'd ask in his gruff tone, "Did ya get my note?"

When he gave me a check ... before cashing it, I would put a teeny tiny note below my neat legible signature on the back. 'I love you dad' Then ... weeks later when his bank statement needed to be calculated he would get my note ... back and forth from one account to the other. Nothing monumental, just a love reminder.

A year after dad died a check written to him arrived in the mail. I was about to sign my dad's name on the back of the check when a flood of memories washed over me ... memories of canceled checks resurfaced. I sat at my desk staring at the check and remembering. I had forgotten ... you find love in the darnedest places. For the last time I signed my dad's name ... then mine below it ... and in teeny tiny printing I added to the back of the check ...'I miss you dad.' And I do.

v

Could I Have This Dance?

A black and white photo ... a small child sitting in a white enamel wash basin outside in the summer sun ... having a bath. There it is ... in full view ... a crippled arm on a smiling baby! A beauty mark that made dad special, unique, not generic. Sometimes when you look at old photos, you're not able to identify who it is. When I see the arm, it makes me smile. Dad's pictures hold something that is uniquely his.

Congenital Birth Defect – that's what they call it now. When he was born it was just plain old 'crippled' ... a thirteen-pound baby with a crippled arm.

As a young boy dad overheard two women talking about his crippled arm. The one woman said to the other woman, "Well ... at least he can always pump gas for a living." A meager prediction that made him determined to prove them wrong. He *did* prove them wrong.

That crippled arm

> ... worked in a quarry and built a house.
> ... could steady a nail while the other did the hammering.
> ... escorted daughters down the aisle.
> ... could hug just fine.

Self-conscious of his crippled left arm ... dad always declined to dance.

But one time ... just once ... I quickly lead him onto the dance floor before he could say NO. I talked as fast as I could to keep his mind off the fact that he was dancing. Finally ... both arms relaxed. Slow music ... the crippled arm ... the reason to not dance faded away. Leaving the floor my dad had a giddy goofy smile and said, "That was nice. I want to do that again."

Joe snapped two photographs of my dad and I dancing that day. They have become my prized possessions.

❋✧❋❋✧❋❋✧❋

Could I Have This Dance? (Part 2)
(John son #1 – 21 yr. old)

Joe and I were going from lounge to lounge, checking out

the different kinds of entertainment that the ship provided. It was boisterous late at night.

I saw John immersed in college age friends and conversation. The Piano bar was loud, as usual. Joe and I decided to stay and 'watch' the night get louder. But once in a while the music would mellow. Taking a moment from his conversation John looked across the room at me and smiled – he pointed to a spot next to the door that was vacant. I nodded. Even though there was no dance floor, we met there. He asked, 'Could I have this dance?' One other son in the room asked his mother to dance as well ... you could almost hear the collective soft sigh from the group as they watched ...

We were queens that night, she and I ... living a moment that would last a lifetime.

School? That's Next Year!

The name of the physician sparked no recognition and I had no reason to believe that it would. As Tommy and I were escorted to the exam room I saw a 'kid' in the hall with a clipboard. I remember thinking 'that can't be the doctor, he looks like he's twelve years old!' Ten minutes later, in walks this twelve-year-old looking doctor.

The discussion was about Tommy's tonsils.

Something familiar kept me looking intently at the doctor's face. If I covered up the mouth on the bottom of his face and the hair on the top of his head and just looked at the eyes & nose, I'd swear that I'd met that man before. But I kept quiet.

The doctor was about to leave the room when I mentioned, "I think you did surgery on my dad." I brought up the St. Cloud Hospital. He nodded with no real recognition until I mentioned 'my dad had Wegener's disease'. (The rarity of dad's disease was like his crippled arm – it distinguished him from others.) The doctor immediately became excited "Yes!" He said "I understand that your dad's eyesight had returned fully in one eye!!" Then he asked, "How is your dad?"

His face dropped when I said dad had died. His reaction to my news was one of failure. What I wanted him to know was totally the opposite of failure. I said to him, "No, no you don't understand … you will never know how much you gave us. His last six months dad could see! He could see his children and wife and grandchildren. The last gift I ever gave my dad was a cane that had elephants carved in the wood and intricate detailing he could *see and touch*. He took his new cane and walked the length of the hallway in his pajamas admiring it. You gave us so much more than you will ever know!"

I told him about the conversation I had with my brother the night they did surgery. After they reported to us what they had done, I turned to my brother and said "Something wonderful happened here tonight … I don't know what … but this surgeon is charged up … excited …" With the use of computers they had been within a millimeter of the optic nerve … and I could tell … something miraculous had happened … and it happened to our dad.

I reminded him that we saw him getting out of the elevator later that night. My mom looked at his young face and commented, "Well, you don't *look old enough* to even be done with school."

Without missing a beat he sweetly put his arm around mom's shoulder and said "School? Oh that's *next* year ... *this year* we're just making money!" He got this worried 80-year-old woman to laugh out loud.

This physician had no idea what he really had added to dad's life. He added sight to his last months ... dad was able to see when the highway patrol pulled us over ... he was able to see and direct me through the streets of St. Cloud ... he was able to sit on the front porch and see the sun. Sight that allowed our dad to see our smiles and our tears ... and gave us the comfort of knowing he could see those who loved him to the last.

As the surgeon left the room that day he said, "You didn't just make my day ... you made my month ... no, you made my six months. That's what medicine is all about, improving the *quality* of life."

Thank you Mr. Twelve-year-old doctor for making something wonderful happen to my dad.

Between Two Worlds

(Location: Dominican Republic)

Everything she described I had seen on TV ... I *thought* I knew what she was talking about. Then she invited me into her life and home ... invited me to step beyond the tourist area into her world ... it was then I realized I knew nothing at all.

I started looking around ... *really looking* ... I saw a world of opposites.

Her house had no doors ... no windows ... sheets hung over the doorways inside to separate the three rooms. After days of rain she walked through mid-calf deep water to get into bed.

Back at the resort; we lounged under grass hut roofs –guests who might have a leak or a drip in their room ... were moved to a different complex.

She cooked something delicious for us - a potato/onion patty. When she put the leftover batter in the refrigerator, I saw what I suspected ... two ... maybe three items inside.

Back at the resort; we chose between three specialty dining rooms or a full buffet.

Her automatic washer is located in front of the power pole outside but it doesn't work right now. The control knob is stripped. (Whirlpool told me they can't send parts into the country.) Clotheslines, too, were nailed to the power pole.

Back at the resort; If I set the dress out of the closet, the next day someone would iron and return it to my room. I told the front desk I was hoping to wear it tonight. In less than five minutes someone delivered an iron.

Her shower is in a cement block out-house, there is no sewer.

Back at the resort; I bathed morning and evening in a tub of hot water.

Her tiny house stands just a few feet from the next house. Most have beds but no other furniture. Her 'street' was like a field road with debris along both sides – scattered chunks of concrete and barbed wire. High unemployment means everywhere people were standing and sitting outside doing nothing.

Back at the resort; People were lounging on the beach doing nothing.

Her house was surrounded by water from the rains ... you could see the mosquitoes ready to hatch.

Back at the resort; a staff mopped marble floors non-stop. We lingered comfortably while the rain kept us prisoners in the lounges and restaurants.

Her haphazard stepping path through the standing water was made from broken chunks of cement.

Back at the resort; a cement sidewalk directed guests to the white sand beaches.

Her neighborhood had dogs that were all skinny. A thin horse pooped in the 'street' where the children play.

Back at the resort; beautiful horses gave carriage rides for guests.

Her children's schools were closed until the water rescinded.

Back at the resort; the golf course was closed until the water rescinded.

Her children must supply paper and pencils to attend school ... many children can not attend.

Back at the resort ... no one knew ...

I thanked her for welcoming me into her home.

I didn't go there to gawk ... or to report what I had seen ... I went there to answer a question I've had for a long time. How much of happiness is dependent on the 'things' we have? Is there happiness in poverty? Is it really the simple things in life that are most extraordinary?

I watched ... and listened. It didn't take long to see her riches

... *her children* ... children with chocolate emerald eyes so magnificent they would make God and Estee Lauder weep at their natural beauty.

... the *people* in her life.

... her *strength*.

... her *hopes* for the future. She takes one class at a time at the university. She's saving to build a house some day. She works at the resort ... steps between two worlds every day.

When she packs her things to move out of this home (and indeed some day she will) – there is much to box up ... a world of love ... a cart full of protectiveness for her children ... a ton of determination.

If I could transplant her family to our world, would I? No

... I would not.

I am afraid she would suffer from our poverty ... our shortage of wisdom ... our absence of appreciation ... our lack of respect for life and one another.

I am afraid she might starve to death here. Her steady diet of appreciating the ordinary would go unfed. I fear that in these remarkable things she will find us lacking ... she will see through our 'stuff' ... find that we have so little compared to her.

I am afraid she will look into our world of antidepressants, searching for the riches of happiness only to find our poverty of the soul.

This world of opposites left me baffled ...

... but I knew when I walked away from that doorless, windowless house, that there are riches in those walls that most people in my world search for all their life ... and never find ...

For additional copies of *Travels on the Yellow Brick Road*

Send requests to:
TRAVELS
1217 Fillmore Street
Alexandria, MN 56308

Book or audio book
$20 plus $5 S & H
Ships in 24 hours.

Or

See www.cathysays.com

About the Author

Cathy Weber-Zunker has been keynoting as well as conducting workshops and training sessions since 1993. Each presentation is an outgrowth of a personal philosophy about life – simple truths – life lessons. Cathy has owned and operated her own home based child care since 1978 in Alexandria, Minnesota. She currently carries an Infant/Toddler license, which enables her to be 'the hand that rocks the cradle'. For information on topics and fees visit www.cathysays.com

Permissions

Annie's Wisdom ... permission granted by Dr. Paul Bergstrand.

Young Legislation ... permission granted by Morris Sulzback.

The Weaver ... permission granted by Tim and Brenda Itzen.

A Different Choice ... permission granted by Mike and Sue Weber.

Richard... permission granted by Richard Towner.

Dalton ... permission granted by Julie and Karl Frovarp.

Margaritaville ... permission granted by Todd and Sherry Bloedel.

Bulla ... permission granted by Jennifer Lee

Gordy ... permission granted by Paul and Julie Altrichter.

Travis' Christmas Wisdom ... permission granted by Nolan and Kathy Kloehn

On saying "I love you" ... permission granted by Joyce Guenther and Dr. Nancy Klepetka

If You Miss Love, You Miss Life ... permission granted by Carol Daniels